IN THE MIDST OF THE STORM

Charles Dickens

Print information available on the last page.

ISBN: 978-1-4907-8299-7 (sc)
ISBN: 978-1-4907-8298-0 (e)

Trafford rev. 05/16/2018

 www.trafford.com

North America & international
toll-free: 1 888 232 4444 (USA & Canada)
fax: 812 355 4082

Praise for *In the Midst of the Storm*

In the midst of my own very real stormy situation in life, it was very fortunate to not only have Charles Dickens's words positively affect my life, but to know the man himself. Powerful stuff indeed!

– Chad R. Goland, Wautoma, Wisconsin

For Royal, Amaris, Milou, Sai, and Vayden, King

The Lord shall bless thee . . . Yea, thou shalt see thy children's children. —Ps 128:5–6

The Bible tells about the dedication of the tabernacle (Nm 7:10–88), the temple (1 Kgs 8:63; Ezr 6:16–18), the Walls of Jerusalem (Neh 12:27), silver and gold (2 Sm 8:11), and private dwellings (Dt 20:5). I would like to also dedicate this work to God and ask for His divine blessing.

I have always told Him, "God, if you bring me out, I will tell it. If you spare my life, I will tell it everywhere I go." I would like to take this opportunity to keep my vow. I would like to thank the God that has been there for me, even when I was a child trapped in a basement storage room with fire blocking the doorway. You were in the fire with me as you were with Shadrach, Meshach, and Abednego. Your Word says, "When you walk through the fire, you will not be burned or scorched, nor will the flames kindle upon you" (Is 43:2, Amplified Bible).

I would like to dedicate this book to the God that was there when I was traveling over 100 miles per hour and came to the end of the road; you provided a highway in the wilderness. I would like to thank the God that was there when the police discharged his weapon at me, missing my head by only inches; the God that was there when I was running and dodging bullets; the God that was there when someone pointed a gun at me at point-blank range and pulled the trigger; and the

God that was there all the times I found myself looking down the barrel of a gun. I am reminded of your Word that says: "Don't forget that I created the metal workers who make weapons [guns] over burning coals. Weapons made to attack you won't be successful" (Is 54:16–17 CEV, emphasis mine). I am forever grateful, "for God has caused me to be fruitful in the land of my affliction" (Gn 41:52).

When David dedicated the house of David to God, he used this Psalm: "I will praise you, Lord! You saved me from the grave and kept my enemies from celebrating my death. I prayed to you, Lord God, and you healed me, saving me from death and the grave . . . I prayed to you, Lord, and in my prayer I said, 'What good will it do you if I am in the grave? Once I have turned to dust, how can I praise you or tell you how loyal you are? Have pity, Lord! Help!' . . . I thank you from my heart, and I will never stop singing your praises, my Lord and my God" (Ps 30:1–3; 8–10; 12).

About the Cover

Mother Nature is the most photographed subject in the world. Storms have captivated people's attention for centuries. Moreover, an astounding eighty six million viewers watch the weather channel regularly. Many storm chasers have even risked their lives to get an up-close photo of a tornado or actual storm.

Uniquely, this cover design was chosen because it symbolizes the many storms of life we have experienced in our lives, specifically for the storms I have experienced in mine. The concept of my standing on the Word gives us a physical illustration of how we must spiritually stand on the Word of God and His promises in the midst of the storm.

Even as the artist painted this cover on his canvas, he experienced storms in his life. He continued to paint through the storm. He explained to me his vision for this cover, and told me that his life was an open canvas, going on to say, "God is continuing to paint a picture in my life."

Additionally, I would like to thank my talented son for designing this awesome book cover. I was able to simply convey my ideas to him over the phone, and he was able to bring them into fruition. In unison with the overall theme for this book, and having observed the many storms I have experienced, he even went as far as to use a font called "Storm" for the words. He is the dedicated owner of Inkjet Graphics.

Contents

Author's Note xiii

Foreword xv

Acknowledgments xxi

Introduction xxiii

Chapter 1   Praise God in the Midst of the Storm 1

   The Show Must Go On 1

   Never Doubt in the Darkness What God Has Shown You in the Light 3

   God Inhabits the Praises of His People 4

   Midnight Praise 5

Chapter 2   Worship God in the Midst of the Storm 9

   Obedience 9

   Faith 10

   Sacrifice 10

Chapter 3   That's Crazy 13

Chapter 4   It's Not Over until God Says It's Over 19

   It's Not Over 19

   Death to the Vision 21

   God's Going to Turn It Around 23

   When Your Dreams and Visions Become Nightmares 24

   The Death to My Vision 25

   The Devil Prompts Us to Fulfill the Vision in Our Own Strength 26

   We Don't Have to Help God, He Is Our Very Present Help 26

   God Is Up To Something 27

   We Should Never Give Up 27

Chapter 5   Against All Odds 29

   Defying the Odds 30

   Rebound 31

Chapter 6   Highs and Lows...33
    When They Go Low, We Go High...34
    450 to 1...35
    Sorry, Wrong Number...35
Chapter 7   Storm Chasers...39
    Man-Made Storms...39
    Let's Cut Right to the Chase...41
Chapter 8   Pray in the Midst of the Storm..43
    Prayer Changes Things...43
    Make It Rain..44
    Partner-Ship (Two Partners in a Ship)..45
    Prayer of Agreement...46
    Discord..46
    Don't Waver in the Storm...46
    Prayer Scriptures..47
    Forgiveness...48
    Prayer for Favor...48
Chapter 9   Sow in the Midst of the Storm...51
Chapter 10   Standing on the Word in the Midst of the Storm..................................55
Chapter 11   Trouble in Paradise...59
    Man-Made Storms...60
    There Is No Place Like Home..60
Chapter 12   The Perfect Storm...65
    Bearing Fruit in the Winter...65
    This Is Only a Test..67
Chapter 13   God Speaks in the Midst of the Storm...69
Chapter 14   The Longest Winter...73
    Angels in the Snow...75
Chapter 15   Your Best Is Yet to Come...79

Final Word The Storm Is over Now...85

Author's Note

Dear valued readers,

Note that the vision for this book was birthed when I was wrongly convicted and received notice that I would be spending the next 360 days in solitary confinement. My amenities would consist of not much more than a metal toilet and sink that were connected, a concrete slab with a makeshift mattress, and a small fogged glass window with no view of the outside world. I had been cut off from modern civilization, and would spend the next year in a brick room the size of a small bathroom. Immediately, I knew I was in the midst of the storm.

Consumer advocacy groups have petitioned the courts, stating that it's unconstitutional, inhumane, and barbaric to keep an individual locked up in those primitive, psychologicaly damaging conditions. Ultimately, I took the attorney general and the Department of Corrections to court pro se (no lawyer, just me and God) and won. "The king's [judges] heart is in the hand of the Lord. Like the rivers of water, He turns it wherever He wishes" (Prv 21 NIV, emphasis mine).

Theodore Roosevelt stated, "Do what you can, with what you have, where you are." Without delay, I took out a piece of paper and begin to write the outline for the chapters of this book. I knew I was going to have to "praise God in the midst of the storm," so I scribbled that down as a chapter.

Correspondingly, as the chapters (storms) of my life were unfolding, I began to write a survival guide for others, "in the midst of the storm."

As a matter of fact, when I look back over my life, I've been through dangers seen and unseen. Nearly thirty years of addiction, having been beat beyond recognition, having had my head stapled up multiple times, and having dived through four glass windows, I can say with all certainty, "I don't look like what I've been through."

The Bible says, "Train up a child in the way he should go, and when he is old, he will not depart from it" (Prv 22:6 NIV). Moreover, from an early age, my mother taught me to call on the name of Jesus. Little did I know then that someday, I would be in the trunk of a car being carried to my death, and I would have to plead the blood of Jesus. Additionally, my parents taught me to do "whatsoever things are true, whatsoever things are honest, whatsoever things are pure."

Please note, this book was comprised with the understanding that "faith is the assurance [the confirmation, the title deed] of the things [we] do not see and the conviction of their reality [faith perceiving as real fact what is not revealed to the senses]" (Heb 11:1 Amplified Bible).

Note also, while you're reading this book, that I give God all the glory for every battle fought and victory won. I still got joy out of all the things I have been through. "It was the best of times, it was the worst of times, it was the age of wisdom, it was the age of foolishness . . . it was the spring of hope, it was the winter of despair . . ." (Charles Dickens).

Foreword

First, I would like to give you a bird's eye view. Eagles have exceptional vision. These seemingly larger-than-life birds use turbulence to reach newer and greater heights in the midst of the storm. In fact, the eagle uses bad circumstances to gain altitudes that they could not have otherwise obtained in good weather. As the eagle rises above the storm, it is able to lock its wings and soar above rain and stormy weather.

Moving forward, I am thankful for the opportunity to be a part of the author's vision for this inspirational book. His real-life experiences and practical teachings encourage readers to spread their wings and rise above the storms of life.

In the midst of the storm, your visibility may be zero, and it may be hard see with clarity how to weather the storm. However, you must never panic because panic leads to failure, and failure is by no means acceptable in this season. You must navigate through the storm with a calm mind. "Thou wilt keep him in perfect peace, whose mind is stayed on thee: because he trusteth in thee" (Is. 26:3).

Note, even as I write, I am in the midst of the storm. We must be confident that we will achieve victory over the storm. "Being confident of this very thing, that He which hath begun a good work in you will perform it until the day of Jesus Christ" (Phil. 1:6).

As an illustration, I once read a book titled *The Eye of the Storm*. In this book, a man was stranded on an island and a hurricane came. In order to survive, he had to grab hold of a tree that was strong enough to withstand the storm. The one thing in particular that caught my attention was that in the middle of the raging winds, the rain ceased for a while, and it was incredibly calm. Meteorologists call this phenomenon the eye of the storm.

This gave the man an opportunity to renew his strength in the onslaught of the storm. We read, "But they that wait on the Lord shall renew their strength; they shall mount up with wings as eagles . . ." (Is. 40:31).

Miraculously, his faith increased in that tree of life since the start of the storm. Holding on to the tree gave him a newfound confidence to prevail over the storm. The storms of life come in all shapes, forms, and fashions. There are storms of depression, addiction, financial instability, loss, and broken relationships to name a few. Whatever the storm may be, know that you can gain confidence in that tree. That tree of life came to save us. He says, "I am the vine ye are the branches: he who abides in Me, and I in him the same bringeth forth much fruit."

The Bible says, "And he [you] shall be like a tree of planted by the rivers of water that bringeth forth his fruit in his season; his leaf also shall not wither; and whatsoever he does shall prosper" (see Psalms 1, emphasis mine).

There was a television show titled *Storm Stories*. The show was based on documentaries of different everyday people who survived extreme weather conditions, such as tornadoes, hurricanes, and storms. These people give a firsthand account of how they survived these harrowing ordeals. Some of their houses were ripped right off the foundations as they clung on for their very lives. I will use this opportunity to share with you my personal storm story/testimony. Note, we can experience victory in the midst of the storm by telling others about the great things that God has done for us. "And they overcame [the enemy] by the blood of the Lamb, and by the words of their testimony" (Revelation 12:11, emphasis mine).

October 23, 2002, there was a brutal attempt on my life. I wasn't a gang member or a murderer but a man who was lost in a world of drugs, lying, and disobedience. Some would have labeled me a hustler, but in God's eyes, I was a purpose waiting to be revealed. Destiny is a rough road, but it takes an undeniable encounter with God to spring you forward into it. The word of God says, "For I know the thoughts that I think towards you saith the Lord, thoughts of peace, and not of evil to give you an expected end" (Jeremiah 29:11).

I was in my home, watching over my three-month-old son, when two gunmen came to my door. I heard a knock, so I grabbed my bag of marijuana and went to the door as usual. The two gunmen portrayed themselves as customers, so I left to fill their order. When I returned, the gunmen pushed their way in. We tussled and fought for about fifteen seconds, when all of sudden, one of them began to shoot. The first bullet startled me, and that's when I could hear my mother's voice. She would say when she got in trouble, she could always call on the name of Jesus.

They continued to fire, and bullet after bullet penetrated my body. As the bullets hit my body, I screamed for Jesus and cried out for God as Peter did when he was sinking in the storm. Matthew 14:30 says, "But when he saw the wind was boisterous, he was afraid; and beginning to sink, he cried Lord save me." The Bible says that, immediately, Jesus stretched fort his hand and caught him. Immediately, Jesus dispatched his holy angels of protection. Goodness and mercy, and the bullets didn't hit any of my vital organs. "For he shall give his angels charge over thee, to keep thee in all thy ways" (Psalms 91:11).

As the final bullets were being dispatched from the gunmen's .357- and .44-caliber guns, bullets hit my body. I felt myself beginning to leave. I faded into darkness and died. While my lifeless body lay there, my mind was still working, and I silently asked God to forgive me for my sins. Immediately, my eyes were opened and life was flowing again through my body.

Some people ask, is there anything too hard for God? The answer is no. The word teaches, "With men this is impossible; but with God all things are possible" (Matthew 19:26). Destiny has a peculiar way of knocking down your door, but when it comes, ready or not, you have to answer. When destiny knocked at my door, I chose life. The word of God says, "Choose you this day whom you will serve" (Joshua 24:15).

When I chose life, I left death where it belonged, defeated by Jesus Christ and through the redemptive work on the cross.

I spent a grueling three days in the intensive-care unit and eight days in the crimes victim unit. I was cut open in the middle of my stomach, my lungs were collapsed, and there were tubes in my nose, mouth, neck and chest. The diagnosis came in. I had sustained multiple gunshots to my body. I had been shot in my neck, rib cage, abdomen, spleen, arms, groin area, and upper and lower back a millimeter away from my upper spine, just two inches away from my neck. According to the doctors' prognosis, my chances of survival were next to none.

I woke up in the ICU, and my parents and younger brother were at my bedside. They were calling on the name of Jesus on my behalf. My eldest brother and the author of this book was incarcerated in Sayre, Oklahoma. My mother informed the prison officials that his little brother had been shot. Just as Joseph was in prison and had favor, he too had favor and was allowed to call home immediately. My parents received my brother's phone call, along with another pastor-and-wife team, who also picked up phones and began to pray. In the midst of the prayer, my brother received a prophetic word from the Lord. My brother began to tell my mother he shall live and not die. He went on to say, "Don't let anyone around my brother who is not speaking life." My mother received the word and did not let anyone who was not speaking life come near me. Proverbs 18:21 declares, "Death and life are in the power of the tongue, and they that love it shall eat the fruit thereof."

Three surgeries were performed, and the doctors' preliminary prognosis was that if I did survive, I would need tracheotomy or colostomy. Chances of survival were looking dim, but God had dispatched his guardian angels who are ministering spirits. Hebrews 1:14 says, "Are they not all ministering spirits, sent forth to minister for them who shall be heirs of salvation?" Miraculously, none of my vital organs were hit, and none of the bullets penetrated my bones.

The Bible tells how Peter was in prison and scheduled to die, "but prayer was made without ceasing of the church unto God for him." The church was praying and believing God to bring Peter out in the same way my church was praying for me. I am a living testimony that the effectual fervent prayer of the righteous availeth much, and "If two of you shall agree on earth as touching anything they shall ask, it shall be done for them of my father which is in heaven" (Matthew 18:19).

Thus, the angel of the Lord appeared to Peter and told him to put on his shoes, loosed his shackles, and let him out of the hands of the enemy. We learn that, Peter "thought he saw a vision" (Acts 12:9). Acts 12:11 says, "And when Peter was come to himself, he said now I know of a surety, that the Lord has sent his angel."

As with the apostle Peter, when I came to myself, I realized that it wasn't a dream and that God had allowed me to walk out of the hospital in just eleven days. I didn't need any life-support mechanisms to live. It was clearly a miracle. Sometimes, when God does miracles, it seems too good to be true or as though you are in a dream. "When the Lord turned again the captivity of Zion, we were like them that dream" (Psalms 121:1).

I am a miracle. I received a gift from God, a second chance at life. We read, when Peter was miraculously released, he knocked on the door of Mary's house, where many were gathered praying for his release. When they heard that Peter was at the door, they didn't believe it, they had to do a double take. The Bible says that when they opened the door, they were astonished. The God I serve will do something so miraculous in your life, you will have to do a double take. When I walked in the church, they had to do a double take.

God showed up and showed out, against all odds, against the doctors' report. Twelve bullets hit my body, but God said that I shall live and not die. God has spared my life for a purpose. That purpose is to tell the world that God is still working miracles. Hebrews 13:8 says, ""Jesus Christ is the same yesterday, today, and forevermore."

My purpose was revealed by destiny knocking at my door. However, it took an undeniable encounter with God to spring me forward into it. I thank God for my storm, and I am a living testimony that if you that if you call on God, he will save you in the midst of the storm.

—Dr. Mario Dickens

Dr. Mario Dickens is the pastor of Victory Temple Church, a ministry committed to reaching the spiritual and tangible needs of the community. He is an entrepreneur, business owner, and publishes a magazine. He has a master's degree as well as a Doctorate of Divinity. He has received numerous prestigious awards and has been featured by television news media outlets for his various works.

Acknowledgments

This book wouldn't have been possible without the prayers and help of many people. First and foremost, a heartfelt thank you goes to my entire family. My parents Elect Lady and Bishop Dickens, for praying without ceasing, and showing by example that love suffers long, is kind, bears all things, hopes all things, and endures all things. I would like to thank my brothers, Mario and Antonio, as well as my sisters, Dana and Kay, for being their brothers' keeper. I am very grateful for my children, Dayshawn and Charles Jr.(Tank); I owe them a great deal of thanks.

A special appreciation to my grandmothers, Emma Owens and Mary Dickens, for being prayer warriors, and praying me through the many storms I faced. The effectual fervent prayer of the righteous availeth much. Thank God for praying grandmothers. I would also like to thank my grandfather, Marshall Owens, for his many words of wisdom throughout the years and his constant encouragement for me to get out and stay out of Lo Debar (a place of no word).

I am thankful to my aunt Sharon, for encouraging me that God is going to turn things around. Also thanks to my aunt Cherie, who prayed me through dangers seen and unseen; my aunt Marsha and godfather Saul, who have always provided unconditional love and support.

A special thanks to a dear friend, Erika Henry, who served as research analyst, providing countless hours of research for this project since its inception. Thanks, Mom, for being my editor and believing in my dream.

Special thanks to Jesse Lewis Gunn for proofreading and pushing me to bring the project to fruition.

I would also like to thank Roosevelt Cardeine for his contributions to this work. I would like to acknowledge the many writers, teachers, evangelists, pastors, preachers, and bishops who have encouraged me throughout the years. While I may not remember all my sources of inspiration over the years, or be able to give you proper recognition, I am now able to encourage others through some of your words of encouragement.

Introduction

In the midst of Superstorm Sandy, Atlantic City and other costal cites were underwater, and the nation's most populous bridges and tunnels were closed. This 800-mile-wide wrath of destruction slammed into the coast with fierce winds and torrential rains, and it rolled back the clock on the twenty-first century as we know it, cutting off modem communication and power to millions of people. Superstorm Sandy tore a path through twenty-four states, killing over one hundred people and causing hundreds of thousands of people to flee their homes. More than one hundred municipalities declared a state of emergency. New Jersey governor Chris Christie said, "I am waiting for the locusts and pestilence next."

All fifty states have declared a state of emergency in the past decade. The storms of life are inevitable. It's not a matter of will the storms of life come, but rather when. If you are reading this book right now, you're most likely preparing to go into a storm, coming out of a storm, or in the midst of the storm. The mariners in the storm with Jonah did not cause the storm, yet they were in the storm (Jonah 1:5). You may not be in a storm, but your family may be going through the storm.

A tropical storm develops when the winds exceed 38 miles per hour, and then the World Meteorological Organization assigns a name to that storm. In the past, the names of these storms have included Andrew, Ivan, Katrina, Matthew, Nicole, Harvey and [your name here]. Storms are associated with barometric minima variously called lows or depressions. Similarly, when we are feeling low and depressed, and the storms of life are raging in our own lives, it seems as though our individual names have been assigned to a storm.

It is not by mere coincidence or chance that you are reading this. God knew every intimate detail about our lives, even before we were born. The Word of God says, "I knew you before you were formed in your mother's womb" (Jer 1:5 NLT). The word "knew" denotes intimacy. When a husband and a wife know each other, they would conceive a child. Genesis 4:1 says, "And Adam knew Eve his wife; and she conceived, and bore Cane." God doesn't make mistakes, and He knew you would need encouragement at this point in your life.

God Is in the Boat with Us

In the midst of the storm, Jesus was in the boat with the disciples. "And he was in the hinder part of the ship" (Mk 4:38). Interestingly, the tiller, helm (controls), and rudder were located in the hinder part of the ship. This clearly lets us know that Jesus was the captain, in control of the ship.

Isaiah 43:2 says, "When thou passest through the waters, I will be with thee, and through the rivers they shall not overflow thee." God is omniscient (all knowing), and knows where you are in the midst of the storm. He is omnipresent (everywhere) and in the boat (storm) with you. God is omnipotent (all powerful) and has the power to bring you out of the storm.

Many of us are faced with what seems to be insurmountable circumstances, leaving us to often wonder, will the devastating storms ever cease? In my personal life, when the storms of life are raging, I can identify with the psalmist David.

"And I said, oh that I had wings like a dove! For then I would fly away, and be at rest. Lo, then I would wander far off, and remain in the wilderness. Selah. I would hasten my escape from the windy storm and the tempest" (Ps 55:6–7).

David was surrounded by his enemies on every side; in the midst of his storm, he hastened his escape. First Corinthians 10:13 lets us know that "God is faithful" and that he will "make a way of escape." This term means literally "an egress or way out." In the early Greek usage, this term had the sense of a landing place for a ship.

"And there arose a great storm of wind, and the waves beat into the ship, so that it was now fall. And he was in the hinder part of the ship, asleep on a pillow: and they awakened him, and said unto him, 'Master, carest thou not that we perish?' And he arose, and rebuked the wind, and said unto the sea, 'Peace, be still.' And the wind ceased, and there was a great calm" (Mk 4:37–39).

Jesus told the disciples, "Let us pass over to the other side." The words "pass over" are from two words meaning to go through. Jesus knew that they were going to go through the storm to get to the other side. He also knows that we are going to go through some storms in our lives.

The Word says, "There arose a great storm." The word "arose" means to come into existence suddenly. This lets us know that the disciples were unsuspecting of the fierce storm. Likewise, we are also caught in the ferocious storms of life, without warning. It is good to know that He is in the boat with us.

Many of us have heard the story of Job. The Bible lets us know that he lost everything in one day. He lost his family, his business, his wealth, and his health. In the midst of Job's storm, he says, "Oh that my words were now written! Oh that they were printed in a book!" (Jb 19:23). Job went on to say "that they were graven with an iron pen and lead in the rock. Forever! For I know my redeemer liveth" (Jb 19:24–25). Job didn't want to wait to find out how the story was going to end. He decided to write in the midst of the storm. He said that he wanted his story engraved in stone so that it could be read for generations to come.

In the midst of the storm, the psalmist wrote, "Write down for the coming generation what the Lord has done so that people not yet born will praise Him" (Ps 102:18 TEV). I decided to write this "in the midst of the storm." I did not want to wait to see how the story ends; I wanted to write a chapter of my life as it was unfolding. I have written portions, when I was wrongly accused and placed in solitary confinement. I have written despite multiple foreclosures. Even as I wrote this introduction, I was being sued for $250,000. There were some chapters in my life that I wish weren't part of my book, but God has allowed me to make a storybook comeback. Without the storms, I would not be the person I am today. I have come to understand that a calm sea does not produce a skilled sailor.

In writing this book, I also was inspired by the apostle Paul who wrote the majority of the New Testament, some of which was written from prison. Despite his sufferings—facing imminent death and being forsaken by many—the apostle Paul continued to write from prison to encourage other believers. Without storms, there would be no Romans, Corinthians, Galatians, Ephesians, Philippians, Philemon, or 2 Timothy, which were written by the apostle Paul while he was in prison. Paul was on a ship, being transferred from one prison to another, when a storm arose. All hope that they should be saved was lost. In the midst of the storm, Paul stood in the midst of them and said, "Wherefore, sirs, be of good cheer, for I believe God that it shall be even as it was told me" (Acts 27:25). In the midst of the storm, we have to believe God.

In the midst of my storm, I continue to write because I believe it shall be as God has spoken. Just like a storm chaser goes in the storm to gather data, I am in the storm, and I have a forecast prediction for you: you are somewhere in the future, and it looks much better than it does right now. Don't be dismayed by the storms—I have heard that every cloud has a silver lining.

Simone Biles is one of the top gymnasts in the world. She is known as the golden girl as a result of her many Olympic gold medals. She was also named athlete of the year in 2016. She has used perseverance to soar above the obstacles in her life, including an early childhood of foster care.

Sports writers confident in her God-given talents have written articles about her victories, amazingly even before her scheduled tournaments. They have told her, "You better do well, the story is already written."

In the same fashion, I would like to encourage you to do well, as it's already written. You are "more than a conqueror" (Rom 8:37). "If God be for [you] us who can be against [you] us," (Rom 8:31, emphasis mine), "no weapon that is formed against thee shall prosper" (Is 54:17). The storm you may be going through shall pass. Your visibility may be near zero, but this too shall pass. Storms and rainy days come in seasons (see Jer 5:24), but seasons must change.

It is written, it is already published, and it is being distributed throughout the world. I can't take it back. "You better do well, the story is already written." You may say, "You don't know my story, you don't know the things that I have been through." I can tell you with full assurance that I have been there, done that, and written a book about it, *In the Midst of the Storm*. Despite criticism, despite incarceration, despite the fact that at times I was my own worst enemy, God was able to draw straight with crooked lines.

Habakkuk 2:3 says, "Write the vision and make it plain on tablets, that he may run who reads it." Experts have suggested that by writing something down, you are 70 percent more likely to remember it. As you navigate through the storms of life, begin to write positive acclimations down, begin to write your goals, dreams, and aspirations, knowing that this too shall come to pass.

Throughout this arduous task, my prayer has been that my speech and preaching be not with enticing words of man's wisdom, but in demonstration of the spirit and power. During the course of writing this book, I would often pray that my pen would be that of a "ready writer" (Ps 45:1), and that I would be able to inspire and encourage others in the midst of the storm.

Charles Dickens

Chapter 1

PRAISE GOD IN THE MIDST OF THE STORM

The Show Must Go On

New York was under siege, and a shutdown of the city was ordered. However, in the midst of Hurricane Sandy, late-night talk show hosts David Letterman and Jimmy Fallon demonstrated that the show must go on. While they didn't have an audience and performed with a quiet monologue, they had a musical band. There was a saying on a plaque that read, "To lead a symphony, you must occasionally turn your back on the crowd."

Oftentimes we find it hard to sing a song of praise in the midst of our trials, and we begin to question God. John had been with Jesus and witnessed the blind receiving their sight, the lame walking, and the dead being raised, but when he was in jail, he sent word stating, "Art thou he that should come, or do we look for another?" (Mt 11:3). John had been with Jesus, but in his time of trouble, he began to doubt the mighty works he had experienced.

Similarly, Ps 137:2 tells the story of when Jerusalem went into Babylonian captivity. The Bible tells of how they hung their harps on the willows. In today's terms, that would simply mean they put them up on the shelf. They felt like in their storm (bondage), they had nothing to sing about, and without a song in their heart, there was no need for instruments. They went on to say, "How shall we sing the Lord's song in a strange place?"

Many times we find ourselves in a *strange* place, and find it hard to praise God in the midst of our trials and storms. We find it strange that everyone else is getting the promotions. Some find it strange that everyone else seems to be happily married, and yet they are estranged from their spouses, leaving many too often wondering, "How shall I sing the Lord's song in a strange place?"

I'm here to tell you that the show must go on. Lights, camera, action! Sometimes when the director is filming, he yells, "Take two." If you don't like how a particular scene of your life is playing out, take two. Take two minutes to give God some praise! He is the director, author, and finisher of your faith. He is able to rewrite the script. He knows the beginning from the end. If you find it hard to praise Him, just begin to look back over your life and all the things that He has brought you through—dangers and snares, seen and unseen. Begin to tell yourself, "If God brought me through that, surely he can bring me through this, because He is the same yesterday today and forever."

Interestingly, I was watching *Good Morning America*, and they showed a clip of R & B pop star Justin Bieber getting tackled onstage by a crazy fan while he was performing and playing the piano. He was knocked down, and the grand piano was overturned, but he got back up and kept performing in front of a live audience. He later tweeted to his millions of followers, "Nothing stops the show." I'm writing to let you know the show must go on! We've been through some things, and may have been knocked down by life, but we must get back up. The show (life) must go on.

Lastly, in Dayton, Ohio, at an air show, a wing walker and the pilot were tragically killed when the airplane crashed. Astonishingly, Jane Wicker, the wing walker, continued to wave at the audience as the plane went down. The tradition of the air show honors those killed by continuing on with the show. They eventually paused for a moment of silence, and then said the show must go on. We have lost some things and some loved ones along the way, but we must go on.

In 1912, the presidential candidate for the progressive party, Theodore Roosevelt, was scheduled to deliver a campaign speech at the Gilpatrick Hotel in Milwaukee, Wisconsin. Immediately before the speech, there was an assassination attempt on his life. The gunman John Schrank was in close range and squeezed the trigger, firing off a shot aimed directly for Roosevelt's heart.

Miraculously, the case for his glasses and manuscript, which was folded up in his shirt pocket, softened the impact of the .32-caliber bullet. He was advised to go to the hospital. Nevertheless, he decided that the show must go on. Theodore Roosevelt suffered a flesh wound. Amazingly, with the bullet still in his body, he approached the podium to deliver his evening speech. During the course of that speech, he managed to pull out the bloody manuscript from his pocket and read from it because the show must go on!

While bleeding and delivering his speech, Theodore Roosevelt stated, "You can't kill me with one bullet." Likewise, the devil has made many assassination attempts against my life. Bullets have flown over my head; I have seen the fire come from the guns, but I declared, "No weapon formed against me shall prosper." People may have tried to assassinate your character, but the Bible says, "People might bring charges against you, but you will prove that they are wrong. Those are the things I do for my servants. I make everything right for them."

As Theodore Roosevelt was running in the presidential race, we also are in a race. Hebrews 12:1 says, "Let us run with endurance the race that was set before us. Looking unto Jesus, the author and finisher of our faith." The show must go on. "The race is not to the swift, or the battle to the strong," but to him that endures to the end. The show must go on; get back up. You have to roll with the punches. In the words of Yogi Berra, "Never give up. It's not over till it's over."

Never Doubt in the Darkness What God Has Shown You in the Light

V. Raymond Edman said, "Never doubt in the darkness what God has told you in the light." In the wake of Superstorm Sandy, the city that never sleeps was without lights. The storm cut power to more than eight million homes, as it rolled back the clock on the twenty-first century and modern civilization as we have come to know it. Broadway, the Lincoln Center, and Carnegie Hall were all in total darkness.

Many of us focus on how dark our circumstances are. However, I've come to realize that it doesn't matter how dark a room is if we turn on our light. Regardless of how dark a world everyone else is living in, if we turn on our light, we can illuminate a room.

Matthew 6:16 says, "Let your light shine before men that they may see your good works, and glorify your Father who is in heaven."

The darkest hour is just before the breaking of day. The Bible declares that Jacob wrestled with God. "And he said, "Let me go, for the day breaketh.' And he said, 'I will not let thee go, except thou bless me'" (Gn 32:26). Jacob had wrestled all night until the breaking of day. In your darkest hour, don't give up; your blessing is on the way. God will turn your p.m. (midnight situation) into an a.m. situation. God says, "I Am that I Am."

God Inhabits the Praises of His People

The Bible says that God inhabits the praises of His people. The Hebrew word for inhabit is *"yasab."* The primitive root here means to sit down, ease the self, dwell, abide, remain, and the like. Essentially, what God is saying is that as you begin to praise Him, he will become one (married) with you. You may ask, "What does that have to do with praise?" If God becomes one with you through your praise, that means that your situation has to change. There is no sickness or depression in God, therefore, as you praise Him, and He becomes one with you, sickness and depression has to leave your body.

You can see this Scripture more clearly in the Amplified Bible. Psalms 22:3 in the Amplified Bible says, "But you are holy, O You, who dwell in [the holy place where] the praises of Israel [are offered]."

When the children of Israel were in the wilderness, they would look over at the enemies of God and see them giving praise to their gods. The enemies of God served Asherah and Baal. These false gods were made from wood. Some scholars believe that their gods resembled a sacred pole made of wood. They wanted to imitate their gods so they would be still. They may have chosen to sit on a stump of wood, but Israel served a living, moving God. "And the Lord went before them by day in a pillar of cloud, to lead them the way; and by night in a fire to give them light to go by, day and night" (Ex 13:21). He went before them in a pillar of cloud in the day and fire at night. We too serve a living God, who's worthy of our praise. We have to praise God in the midst of the storm, in the midst of our enemies. On the night that Jesus was betrayed, He gave thanks (see I Cor 11:24).

Jahaziel received a word from the Lord as follows: "Thus saith the Lord unto you, 'Be not afraid nor dismayed by reason of this great multitude; for the battle is not yours, but God's.'" There is something about getting a word from God in the midst of the storm. A word aptly spoken is like apples of gold in settings of silver (Prv 25:11 NIV). And how delightful is a timely word! (Prv 15:23 NAS).

The word goes on to say, "Ye shall not need to fight in this battle: set yourselves, stand ye still, and see the salvation of the Lord with you. O Judah and Jerusalem: fear not, nor be dismayed; tomorrow go out against them, for the Lord will be with you" (2 Chr 20:17).

And when he had consulted with the people, he appointed singers unto the Lord that should praise the beauty of holiness as they went out before the army, and to say, 'Praise the Lord, for His mercy endureth for ever.' And when they began to sing and to praise, the Lord set ambushes against the children of Ammon, Moab, and mount Seir, which were come against Judah, and they were smitten" (2 Chr 20:21–22).

Jehoshaphat appointed the Tribe of Judah to go before the army praising God. Judah means praise. You can accomplish great victories by praising God. It is one thing to pray, but when you begin to praise God, you are saying, "God, I thank you in advance for the outcome." The lyrics to a popular hymn says, "Don't wait until the battle is over; shout now, because in the end we're going to win."

As Judah was praising God and singing, "Praise the Lord, for His mercy endureth forever," God set ambushers, and Jehoshaphat's enemies all killed each other. When Jehoshaphat and his army went to survey the situation, there was nothing but dead bodies and riches. There was such an abundance of precious jewelry, clothing, and valuables that, "they were three days gathering the spoil because it was so much" (2 Chr 20:25).

We praise God in the midst of the storm, knowing that He is able to calm the storm. Psalms 107:29 says, "He maketh the storm calm so that the waves thereof are still."

Not only did God deliver Jehoshaphat from his enemies, but he blessed him exceedingly as well. Ephesians 3:30 says, "Now unto Him who is able to do exceeding abundantly above all that we ask or think according to the power that worketh in us."

Midnight Praise

The Bible says, "And at midnight Paul and Silas prayed, and sang praises unto God and the prisoners heard them. And suddenly there was a great earthquake, so that the foundations of the prison were shaken. And immediately all the doors were opened, and everyone's bands were loosed" (Acts 16:25). When you begin to praise God in the midst of the storm, your circumstances will begin to change suddenly! It doesn't matter how dark your situation is, the darkest hour is just before the break of day.

Interestingly enough, had not Paul and Silas been in prison, the jailor and his family would have not been saved. I can remember being in prison in Sayre, Oklahoma, and the unit manager addressed the unit and began to tell the inmates how he wanted us to officiate his memorial after his death. He was certain that he only had a short time left to live. Several other inmates and I invited him in the back room of the chapel for prayer. We laid hands on him in faith. He miraculously recovered, and I passed him a while later in the prison yard, and he said, "How are you doing, preacher?"

The darkest hour is just before the breaking of day. The Bible declares that Jacob wrestled with God. "And he said let me go, for the day breaketh. And he said I will not let thee go except thou bless me" (Gn 32:26). Jacob had wrestled all night, until the breaking of day. In your darkest hour, do not give up. Your blessing is on the way.

One of the chapel visitors stood in front of the prison congregation and said that he had a vision that the inmates were not trying to break out of the prison, but rather the people outside of the barbwire fences were trying to break into the prison because of the anointing on the inside. I believe that like in the days of Obadiah (see 1 Kgs 18:4), God still had some prophets in caves (prisons).

We have to come to the realization that it is not all about us. Joseph went to the pit and to prison to save his family. The Bible lets us know that he went before them, and when there was a famine in the land, he was in a position that he was able to provide for them.

I believe that Jesus Christ is the same yesterday, today, and forever. What I am trying to say is that I believe if He did it in the Bible days, He can do it today. I was listening to an old sermon by Martin Luther King Jr. He began to talk about how strange things happen at midnight. I have even heard my own father preach about midnight. Dr. Martin Luther King Jr. said it best, "I say to you today my friends, that in spite of the difficulties and frustrations of the moment, I still have a dream."

The Bible says as Paul and Silas were praising God, "Immediately all the doors were opened." I am a witness that as you begin to praise God, He will immediately begin to open doors in your life. Doors of opportunities, doors of prosperity, doors of deliverance, doors of freedom, and doors that no man can close. There is deliverance in your praise. The Word says, "And at midnight Paul and Silas prayed, and sang praises unto God; and the prisoners heard them. And suddenly . . ." As you begin to praise God, things begin to suddenly happen in your life.

The name Jacob meant conman, trickster, or deceiver. However, Jacob wrestled until God changed his name. Jacob's name was changed to Israel, which means "friend of God." God has a blessing with your name on it. Many of life's failures are from people who did not realize how close they were to success when they gave up. The struggle is what makes success. Don't throw in the towel; God has the ability to turn your midnight situation (p.m.) into an "a.m." situation. When God appeared to Moses in the burning bush, and Moses questioned His name, God stated, "I AM . . ."

"I *am* the bread of life; he who comes to Me shall never hunger, and he who believes in Me shall never thirst" (Jn 6:35).

"I *am* the light of the world; he who follows Me shall not walk in the darkness, but shall have the light of life" (Jn 8:12).

"I *am* the door; if anyone enters through Me, he shall be saved, and go in and out and find pasture" (Jn 10:9).

"I *am* the true vine, and my Father is the vinedresser. Every branch in Me that does not bear fruit, He takes away; and every branch that bears fruit, He prunes it, that it may bear more fruit" (Jn 15:1–2).

In sum, the dictionary defines *a.m.* as "the time from midnight to noon." Additionally, the abbreviations *a.m.* stand for the Latin phrase *ante meridiem,* meaning "before noon." I know the storm clouds may be darkest right now, and the enemy may be trying to get you to throw in the towel. Nevertheless, remember the difference from midnight to morning is only sixty seconds. The psalmist went on to say, "Weeping may endure for a night, but joy comes in the morning [a.m.]."

"I **am** the good shepherd; the good shepherd lays down His life for the sheep . . . I am the good shepherd, and I know My own, and My own know Me" (Jn 10:11, 14). And "I **am** the resurrection and the life; he who believes in Me shall live, even if he dies" (Jn 11:25).

"I am the way, the truth, and the life; no one comes to the Father but through Me" (Jn 14:16).

Chronicles 20:21 tells the story of Jehoshaphat, who went to war against multiple armies. People told him, "A huge army is coming from Edom to fight against you" (2 Chr 20:2 NIV). By all accounts, he was in a storm. His enemies had risen up against him. Jehoshaphat began to fast and call a solemn assembly fasting. Additionally, he began to P.U.S.H., the acronym meaning "Pray until something happens." Jehoshaphat prayed as follows: "We don't know what to do. But we're looking to you to help us."

Chapter 2

WORSHIP GOD IN THE MIDST OF THE STORM

There comes a time when we must worship God in the midst of the storm. We praise God for the wonderful things He has done for us, and the many blessings He has bestowed on us. However, we worship God for who He is, and His many attributes. Unlike praise, worship requires extreme obedience, faith, and sacrifice. Initially, we can learn for Abraham's unquestioning obedience as follows:

Obedience

"And it came to pass after these things, that God did tempt [test] Abraham and said unto him, 'Abraham: behold, here I am.' And He said, 'Take now thy son Isaac, whom thou lovest, and get thee into the land of Moriah; and offer him there for a burnt offering upon the mountains which I will tell thee of'" (Gn 22:1–2, emphasis mine).

Next, this act of worship required faith. Abraham notified his servants that he and his son were going to worship and would come back. Abraham knew that others were not prepared to go an altitude in worship as he was. Occasionally, your critics will come on the scene and say you are going too far with praise and worship stuff, saying things like, "It doesn't take all that." What they fail to understand is that if you have been delivered much, you praise much. Furthermore, they were not there when God brought you out!

Courageously, when Abraham went to worship, he told the young men to stay "with the ass." I am going to worship and will be back. *Merriam-Webster's Dictionary's* definition of *ass* is a donkey or fool. If they want to remain with the fools, that's okay, but you have to make up in your mind. I am going to worship. As for me and my house, we will praise the Lord. "I will bless the Lord at all times; His praise shall continually be in my mouth." Abraham understood this concept through the portals of time, thousands of years ago. This can be seen clearly in the following passage:

Faith

"Then on the third day, Abraham lifted up his eyes and saw the place far off. And Abraham said unto the young men, 'Abide ye here with the ass; and I and the lad will go yonder and worship, and come again'" (Gn 22:4–5).

Subsequently, worship takes extreme sacrifice. The Bible tells the story of the woman that anointed Jesus with expensive perfume. She cried at the feet of Jesus. Her tears wet His feet, and she wiped them with her hair. She kissed them and went on to pour the expensive perfume on them (Lk 7:36–38). Biblical scholars have estimated that the perfume she poured on His feet was equivalent to one year's wages. We learn from this encounter that worship took extreme sacrifice on the part of the sinful woman. However, because of her sacrifice, Jesus said to her, "Your sins are forgiven."

Sacrifice

"And they came to the place which God had told him of, and Abraham built an altar there, laid wood in order, bound Isaac his son, and laid him on the altar of wood. And Abraham stretched out his hand and took the knife to slay his son. But the angel of the Lord called to him from heaven and said, 'Abraham, Abraham!' And He said, 'Do not stretch out your hand against the lad, and do nothing to him, for now I know that you fear God, since you have not withheld your son, your only son, from Me.' Then Abraham raised his eyes and looked, and behold, behind was a ram caught in the thicket by his horns. Abraham went and took the ram, and offered him up for a burnt offering in the place of his son. And Abraham called the place Jehova-Jireh. The Lord will provide, as it is said this day, 'in the mount of the Lord it will be provided'" (Gn 22:9–14).

Seeing that Abraham began to worship in obedience, faith, and sacrifice, God provided a ram in the bush (a way out). Similarly, as you begin to model Father Abraham's prerequisite for worship, God will make a way out where there seems to be none in your life. He will provide a ram in the bush. Moreover, Abraham named that place Jehovah-Jireh, meaning "The Lord will provide." Abraham built an altar to God and used it as a memorial of testament so if he ever passed back by that place, he could remember the mighty acts of God. I'm sure after that experience, Abraham knew God as Jehovah-Jireh, his provider. We also have to look back over our lives and recall the things that God has done for us. We have to remember that He has also been Jehovah-Jireh in our lives; He has made a way out of no way.

"So the people grumbled at Moses, saying, 'What shall we drink?' Then he carried out to the Lord, and the Lord showed him a tree, and he threw it into the waters, and the waters became sweet. There He made for them a regulation, and there He tested them.

And He said, 'If you will give earnest heed to the voice of the Lord your God, and do what is right in His sight, and give ear to His commandments, and keep all His statutes, I will put none of these diseases on you which I have put on the Egyptians. For Lord I am, Jehovah, your healer'" (Ex 15:24–26).

"When Gideon saw that he was an angel of the Lord, he said 'Alas, O Lord God! For now I have seen the angel of the Lord face to face." And the Lord said to him, 'Peace to you, do not fear. You shall not die.' Then Gideon built an altar to the Lord and named it Jehovah Shahlom, the Lord is peace" (Judg 6:22–24).

"So Moses said to Joshua, 'Choose men for us, and go out, fight against Amalek. Tomorrow I will station myself on top of the hill with the staff of God in my hand.' And Joshua did as Moses told him, and fought against Amalek; and Moses, Aaron, and Hur went up to the top of the hill. So it came about when Moses held his hand up that Israel prevailed, and when Moses let his hands down, Amalek prevailed. But Moses's hands were heavy. Then they took a stone and put it under him, and he sat on it. And Aaron and Hur supported his hands, one on one side and one on the other. Thus his hands were steady until the sun set. So Joshua overwhelmed Amalek and his people with the edge of the sword. Then the Lord said to Moses, 'Write in a book as a memorial, and recite it to Joshua that I will utterly blot out the memory of Amalek from under heaven.' And Moses built an altar, and named it Jehovahnissi, the Lord is my banner" (Ex 17:9–15).

"But as for you, speak to the sons of Israel, saying, 'You shall surely observe my Sabbaths, for this is a sign between Me and you throughout your generations, that you may know that I am Jehovah-M'kaddesh, the Lord who sanctifies you'" (Ex 31:13).

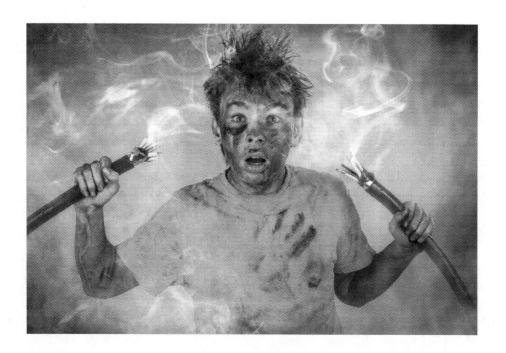

Chapter 3

THAT'S CRAZY

There is a saying that says, "That's crazy." Turn on the television, and you will hear movie stars saying, "That's crazy." Watch sports, and when the players don't agree with the call, they'll say, "That's crazy." Turn on the news, and you may hear the news anchor saying, "That's crazy."

Watch a Chevy commercial, and you will hear, "That's crazy." I was watching *Preachers of L.A.*, and one of the preachers said, "That's crazy." On your job, you may hear your coworkers saying, "That's crazy," and more than likely you yourself may have said, "That's crazy." For example, *World News* reported that Snow Mountain was closed because of snow. That's crazy.

The apostle Paul explained: "But God has chosen the foolish things of the world to confound the wise, and God has chosen the weak things of the world to confound the things which are mighty" (1 Cor 1:27).

With more than 750 Halls of Fame in America, Noah made it to the most important one, "The Faith Hall of Fame" (Heb 11). The Word teaches: "By faith, Noah built a ship in the middle of dry land. He was warned about something he couldn't see, and acted on what he was told" (Heb 11:7).

When one thinks about all the circumstances surrounding Noah and the building of the ark, one can't help but to come to the conclusion, "That's crazy."

It took Noah 120 years to build the ark, with no forecast of rain in sight. As a matter of fact, Noah built the ark having never seen rain in his life. Genesis 2:5–6 lets us know that prior to the flood, water came from the ground up.

I'm sure that for 120 years, as he was building this giant ship, people were saying, "That's crazy." Noah continued to build the ark even though he was hundreds of miles away from the nearest ocean. Noah continued to build, despite the naysayers, despite of his critics. I'm sure they whispered, "That' s crazy," just loud enough for Noah to hear them. I'm sure his neighbors ridiculed him and called him crazy as he was building this giant ship in his front yard.

The ark was six times longer than it was wide, the size of one and a half football fields, and as high as a four-story building. Some experts have estimated that the ark could hold the equivalent in weight of eight hundred railroad cars. When you consider the time and era, and that there were no modern tools available, that's crazy, how someone could saw thousands and thousands of planks made out of gopher wood.

God's thoughts are not our thoughts, and His ways are not our ways. He chooses the foolish things of the world to confound the wise. I went to hear a speaker speak; he is the founder of Preacher Boy Jeans. As I listened, he told the story of how Matthew 6:6 said, "But when thou prayest, enter into thy closet." He said he didn't know any better, so he went into his literal closet to pray.

He started a clothing line called Preacher Boy Jeans. He is now a multimillionaire, and his clothing line is international. He stated that he only had an eighth-grade education but was invited to speak to large corporations and to Harvard University. I will be the first to say, just like *The Beverly Hillbillies*. He recounted how he loaded up and moved to Beverly Hills. That's crazy!

I need only to look at the life of my own family to see how God chooses the foolish things of the world to confound the wise. Although my mother only had a high school diploma, others in her profession had master's degrees and doctorates. She worked for a Fortune 500 company and quickly excelled to the top. The media noted her many accomplishments. As the top account executive, she sold some of the biggest accounts in her corporation's history. She was the lead executive representing her firm in the mid-nineties, when the first health care joint venture was formed in Wisconsin to include a private employer, a health care system, and city and county partners. This was historic! My mother was responsible for half of all the major businesses in southeastern Wisconsin and all the city and public sectors. She flew in and out of the country, meeting with high-ranking executives, presidents, and CEOs of various Fortune 500 companies.

She sat in the General Motors boardroom and looked up at the sky through a glass ceiling. That's crazy!

Interestingly, before I could finish writing this book, my mom received an honorary doctorate degree. Comparatively, just as First Lady Michelle Obama spoke of presidential candidate Hillary Clinton, my mother "has the guts and the grace to keep coming back and putting those cracks in the highest and hardest glass ceiling until she finally breaks through, lifting all of us along with her."

I was placed in solitary confinement for writing and profiting off my first book in prison. The captain told me that he had seen my book being sold on the Internet. I regrettably responded, "Buy a copy then." As a result, I was sentenced to the maximum time a human can be kept in those primitive conditions by law. However, this gave me more time to start writing another book, *In the Midst of the Storm*. You're reading it right now, and that's crazy. I wrote the warden and told him my book would be "distributed throughout the world" regardless of their futile efforts to stop me. I was released out of the "hole" (solitary confinement) almost a year later and returned to the normal prison population.

To summarize, I made a phone call, and someone told me my book was rated five stars and was being sold in the United Kingdom for euros. I had to do some research to determine the value of a euro, and now my book is also available at Walmart. That's crazy.

Additionally, I ordered a financial book while in prison from an author who became my favorite. While I was in prison, the same author wrote a review on my financial book, stating, "This book is nice and worth the money." I was in jail and just found out that my book had sold thousands and thousands of copies. I give God all the glory, but I can't help but say, that's crazy.

Many years ago, I went to the prison chaplain and let him know that I had a word to preach. I explained to him that I wanted to share it with the church. He responded by asking me what Bible College I went to. I told him I have not been to Bible College. He then asked where I went to seminary. I explained that I didn't attend any seminary either. He let me know that there was no way that I would be allowed to get up and speak. I remember, after our meeting, walking down the long hall of the prison questioning God and feeling belittled, embarrassed, and ashamed.

However, on that following Sunday morning, I went to church, and there was a guest speaker. We were praising and worshipping God. The speaker looked at me and said that the Holy Spirit told him to give me the microphone. I gladly received the microphone, and went on to encourage the other men. That's crazy. When God has a word to get out, nothing or no one can stop it from coming forth. He said, "So shall my word be that goeth forth out of my mouth. It shall not return unto me void, but it shall accomplish that which I please. and it shall prosper in the thing whereto

I sent it" (Is 55: 11). Since that situation, I have been to seminary, have had a degree in theology, certifications, and credentials. And that's crazy.

The Bible tells the story of a gang member named Jephthah who was the son of a harlot. "And Gilead's wife bore him sons, and his wife's sons grew up and thrust out Jephthah, and said unto him, 'Thou shalt not inherit in our father's house, for thou art the son of a strange woman.' Then Jephthah fled from his brethren and dwelt in the land of Tob, and there were vain men to Jephthah, and went out with him" (Judg 11:2).

"When it came time for them to go to war, they sent for Jephthah. Jephthah said unto them, 'Did not ye expel me out of my father's house? And why are ye come unto me now when you are in distress?'" (Judg 11:5). God has a way of turning your situation around. I'm here to tell you, it's crazy out there—one minute people will hate you, and the next minute they will need your assistance. Remember to close your doors softly. You never may know when you will have to come back through that door.

While "That's crazy" has become a common saying of twenty-first century, I believe the term was coined BC. When God would perform miracles back then like he does now, people would say, "That's crazy." For example, this age-old adage was used around AD 37, when the Bible says that Peter was in prison and due to be executed in the morning. When God miraculously brought him out of prison and he showed up at the door where they were praying, Rhoda came to the door. She ran and told everyone Peter was at the door. "You are crazy!" everyone told her. "But she kept saying that it was Peter. Then they said it must be his angel" (Acts 12:15 CEV).

Many of them said, "He has a demon in Him! He is crazy! Why listen to Him?" (Jn 10:20 CEV). If they called Jesus crazy, they will call you crazy also. God is capable of doing some things in your life where those around you will say, "That's crazy. In their natural understanding, they won't be able to comprehend how you got the job, how you got the promotion, how you got the house, or why you are so blessed. God will even do things in your life that will leave you saying, "That's crazy."

George Washington Carver said, "When you can do the common things of life in an uncommon way, you will command the attention of the world."

Chapter 4

IT'S NOT OVER UNTIL GOD SAYS IT'S OVER

It's Not Over

"Peter therefore was kept in prison, but prayer was without ceasing of the church unto God for him" (Acts 12:5). The word "but" negates everything that was previously said. It didn't matter that Peter was in prison, because the Word says "but prayer." We have been in some situations, but prayer! It may have seemed liked there was no way out, but God! This passage from Acts explains: "And when he would have brought him forth the same night, Peter was sleeping between two soldiers, bound with two chains; and the keepers before the door kept the prison" (Acts: 12:6).

Why was Peter able to sleep so peacefully on death row the night before he was going to be executed? The late Bishop G. E. Patterson was preaching and jokingly said that he would have been worrying and pacing the floor all night, dragging around the soldiers that were chained to him. I think if I were in a situation where I am face execution, I would be planning my escape; but when you have a promise from God, you are able to sleep like Peter in the midst of the storm.

The Bible lets us know that Peter had a promise that he would not die until he was an old man. In Acts 12, he was still a young man, therefore he knew that regardless of how the situation looked, it was not over. He had a promise. John 21:18–19 reminds us of that promise: "Verily, verily, I say unto thee, when thou was young, thou girdest thyself, and walkest whither thou wouldest. But when thou shalt be old, thou shalt stretch forth thy hands, and another shall gird thee, and carry thee wither thou wouldest not. This spake he, signifying by what death he should glorify God."

It's not over until God says it's over. It doesn't matter how bad the situation looks. I was in prison in Sayre, Oklahoma, hundreds of miles from my hometown of Milwaukee, Wisconsin. A good friend and brother in Christ, Brother David Morell, came and told me that I needed to go to the chaplain's office. I asked him why, and he didn't respond. I somehow could sense that something was wrong. When I got to the chaplain's office, he began to inform me that my brother had been shot multiple times and that it didn't look good.

The chaplain informed me that I could call home. I called my mother, and she began to tell me that my brother had been shot. She told me that they had to cut him open and that he was so swollen that they couldn't close him back up. I told her, "Let's pray." I prayed until the chaplain ran out of the office. I continued to pray, and suddenly I received a word from God. I heard something in my spirit say, "This sickness is not unto death, but that God may be glorified." I instantly stopped praying, and I told my mother that I got a word from God. I told her, "This sickness is not unto death, but that God may be glorified." I went on to inform her not to let anyone around my brother speak negatively.

I walked back to my unit and told my roommate what happened. I lay facedown on the concrete floor, stretched out, and began to pray and cry out to God. I remembered the word that God had given me, so before I went to sleep, I opened the Bible to John 11:4, which says, "This sickness is not unto death, but for the glory of God, that the Son of God might be glorified thereby."

Later that night, I placed the Bible close to my bed and went to sleep. The enemy came in the midnight hour and began to try to get me to doubt the Word of God. The devil began to try to tell me that my brother was going to die. I was not ignorant concerning his vices, so I woke up and told the devil, "He's not going to die." I told the enemy to look at the Word; I pointed to Bible that was opened to John 11:4 and said, "This sickness is not unto death, but that God may be glorified." I went back to sleep, just as Peter was sleep chained to the soldiers when he was due to die in the morning. When you get a word from God, you can sleep like a baby. In the midst of the storm. I'm here to tell you that it's not over until God says it's over.

There was a bishop of the Greek Orthodox Church who was on an airplane seated next to a woman. The airplane began to experience difficulties and began to shake violently. The woman seated next to the bishop began to scream and yell, "We are all going to die." The bishop said,

"Shut up, silly woman. We are not going to die. I am on this plane, and I got a promise from God. There are some things that God has promised me that have not yet come to pass, therefore I can't die. You better be glad that I am on this plane. God is not a man that He should lie. If God has promised you some things in your life, they must come to pass."

Death to the Vision

If God has given you a vision, you may experience death to the vision. This is the period when it seems like the vision is not going to come to pass. This is the time when people will begin to tell you that you are out of your mind. This is the period when it seems as though the dream and vision has clearly died. The Bible illustrates this principle:

"Verily, verily, I say unto you, except a corn of wheat fall to the ground and die, it abideth alone. But if it die, it bringeth forth much fruit" (Jn 12:24).

Isaiah 6:1 says, "In the year that King Uzziah died, I saw the Lord." The Hebrew word for "saw" is *raah,* meaning "to see clearly." Sometimes we can't truly see God until things begin to die in our own lives. We have to begin to die with our own selfish ambitions.

There were twenty-one men in the Bible who received visions from God. Abraham was the first the one.

"After these things, the word of the Lord came to Abraham in a vision, saying, 'Fear not, Abraham. I am thy shield, and thy exceeding great reward.'

"And Abraham said, 'Lord God, what wilt thou give me, seeing I go childless, and the steward of my house is Elizezer of Damascus?'

"And behold, the word of the Lord came unto him, saying, 'This shall not be thine heir, but he that shall come forth out of thine own bowels shall be thine heir.'

"And He brought him forth abroad and said, 'Look now toward the heaven, and tell the stars, if thou be able to number them.' And He said unto him, 'So shall thy seed be.'

"And he believed in the Lord; and he counted it to him for righteousness" (Gn 15:1–6).

We can see the death of the vision in the life of Abraham and Sarah. God promised Abraham he would have a child when he was one hundred years old, and his wife would be ninety. Abraham believed that God was able to perform that which He promised.

God will give you a vision that seems so far out of your reach, all you can do is laugh. You will ask yourself, "Am I being punked [made fun of]? Where are the television cameras? This has got to be a practical joke. This has got to be some crazy reality show."

But God has chosen the foolish things of the world to confound the wise, and God has chosen the weak things of the world to confound the things which are mighty (1 Cor 1:27).

When God told Sarah that she was going to have a baby in her old age, all she could do was laugh. She couldn't comprehend it. God will miraculously do things in your life that you may not understand, and when you try to figure it out in your finite mind, all you can do is laugh.

Then Abraham fell on his face and laughed, and said in his heart, "Shall a child be born unto him that is a hundred years old? And shall Sarah that is ninety years old bear?" (Gn 17:17).

The conclusion of the story was that after Abraham's vision died, God brought it back to life. "For Sarah conceived and bore Abraham a son in his old age, at the set time of which God had spoken unto him" (Gn 21:2). "And Abraham was a hundred years old when his son Isaac was born unto him. And Sarah said, 'God hath made me to laugh, so that all that hear will laugh with me" (Gn 21:5–6).

The vision provides us with the necessary motivation not to become discouraged while we are waiting for God to bring it to pass. Additionally, the vision produces character in us and develops patience, meekness, and self-control, and increases our faith. God is far more concerned about our longevity. God knows that our anointing will take us where our character can't keep us.

Some have called the period of waiting for the vision to come to pass as "the dark night of the soul." I believe that when Abraham began to become discouraged, and his situation seemed bleak and dark, all he had to do was look up at the stars in the dark sky and remember the vision.

For Abraham, human reason for hope being gone, hoped in faith that he should become the father of many nations, as he had been promised, so numberless shall his descendants be.

He did not weaken in faith when he considered the utter impotence of his own body, which was as good as dead because he was about a hundred years old, or when he considered the barrenness of Sarah's deadened womb.

No unbelief or distrust made him waver (doubtingly question) concerning the promise of God, instead he grew strong and was empowered by faith as he gave praise and glory to God, fully satisfied and assured that God was able and mighty to keep His word and do what He had promised (Rom 4: 18–21 AMP).

God gave Joseph a dream. "And Joseph dreamed a dream, and he told it to his brethren, and they hated him yet the more" (Gn 37:5). "And he dreamed yet another dream and told it to his brethren, and said, 'Behold, I have dreamed a dream more. And behold, the sun and the moon and the eleven stars made obeisance to me'" (Gn 37:9).

The Bible went on to say, "And they took him and cast him into a pit" (Gn 37:24). Joseph was sold by his brothers to the Midianites, who in turn sold him to Potiphar. "And Joseph's master took him, and put him into the prison, a place where the king's prisoners were bound. And there he was in the prison" (Gn 39:20).

In Joseph's dream, there were no pits or prisons. When God gives us a vision, he doesn't show us everything that's betwixt and between the prophecy and the promise. He doesn't let us know that there are some things that we are going to have to go through before the promise is fulfilled. God doesn't show us the pits and the prisons.

We can see in the life of Joseph that in spite of the circumstances that Joseph had to endure, the Lord was with him. Genesis 39:21 says, "But the Lord was with Joseph, and showed him mercy, and gave him favor in the sight of the keeper of the prison." When we feel like we are at rock bottom, the pits, the lowest point in our lives, or the depths of despair, God is with us.

God's Going to Turn It Around

Joseph went from the prison to the palace in one day. God is also able to turn your situation around in twenty-four hours. "Then Pharaoh sent and called Joseph. And they brought him hastily out of the dungeon, and he shaved himself and changed his raiment, and came unto Pharaoh" (Gn 41:14). "And Pharaoh said unto Joseph, 'See, I have set thee over all the land of Egypt.' And Pharaoh took off his ring from his hand, and put it on Joseph's hand, and arrayed him in vestures of fine linen, and put a gold chain about his neck" (Gn 41:41–42).

That which the enemy meant for evil, God has a way of turning around for your good. Joseph went from prison to the palace in twenty-four hours. He told his brothers, "But as for you, ye thought evil against me. But God meant it unto good, to bring to pass, as it is this day, to save much people" (Gn 50:20).

The Bible lets us know about a famine that was so severe that people were paying silver for horse heads and dove droppings. They were so hungry that one woman said, "Give thy son, that we may eat him today, and we will eat my son tomorrow" (2 Kgs 6:28).

"And there was a great famine in Samaria. And behold, they besieged it, until an ass's head was sold for fourscore pieces of silver, and the fourth part of a dove's dung for five pieces of silver" (2 Kgs 6:25).

However, Elisha the prophet of God came on the scene and said, "Hear ye the word of the Lord. Thussaith the Lord, tomorrow about this time shall a measure of fine flour be sold for a shekel, and two measures of barley for a shekel, in the gate of Samaria" (2 Kgs 7:1).

I remember being incarcerated and receiving a letter from my aunt Sharon. In the letter, she began to tell me to get ready to read because "God is going to turn it around." I continued to read the letter, and she began to give me instructions to "stand up and begin to turn around." As I began to turn around, I began to get excited, because I believed God was turning things around in my life. Singer and songwriter Fred Hammond said, "Late in the midnight hour, God's going to turn it around, it's going to work in your favor."

When Your Dreams and Visions Become Nightmares

Like Job, we also come to a place in our lives where our dreams and visions become nightmares. Job had dreams and visions about his family, business, and children's future.

We know that he woke up early in the morning and offered sacrifices for them. He was a successful businessman, and I am sure that he had dreams for his future.

Likewise, we have dreams and visions for our families, businesses, and our lives. While the Sabeans may not have taken our children away with the edge of the sword like they did Job's, our children may have been carried off to prison, or be in bondage to drugs and alcohol.

Job received notice that all his ten children had been killed. Job said, "When I say my bed shall comfort me, my couch shall ease my complaint, then thou scarest me with dreams, and terrifies me through visions" (Job 7:13–14). Similarly, when God gives us a vision, He doesn't show us everything between and betwixt the prophecy and the promise. There is a time when it feels like our dreams and visions have become nightmares. We have to come to realize that there has to be *A Nightmare on Elm Stree*t if we want the sequel to be a *Miracle on 34th [place your street here].*

The apostle Paul said in Philippians 1:6: "Being confident of this very thing that he which hath begun a good work in, you will perform it until the day of Jesus Christ." If God started work on you, He will perform it. It's not over until God says it's over.

I was watching *World News*, and Victoria Duval was playing tennis in the US Open. Amazingly, she won the first round and defeated her opponent with an upsetting victory. When the news reporter interviewed her and her brother, her brother was wearing a T-shirt that had the letters *DON* in large, bold print. He went on to say that the initials stood for "Dreams over Nightmares." We have to begin to put our dreams over our nightmares. I know we may face some scary situations, and it might seem as though there is no way out.

If it seems as though your dreams and visions are not going to come to pass, remember that there has to be death to the vision. If it is a God-given vision, it will surely come to pass. "God is not a man, that He should lie" (Nm 23:19). "For the vision is yet for an appointed time, but at the end it shall speak and not lie. Though it tarry, wait for it, because it will surely come, it will not tarry" (Hb 2:3).

The Living Bible of Habakkuk 2:3 reads: "These things I plan won't happen right away. Slowly, steadily, surely, the time approaches when the vision will be fulfilled. If it seems slow, do not despair, for these things will surely come to pass. Just be patient! They will not be overdue a single day!"

The Death to My Vision

I was in the North Fork Correctional Facility in Sayre, Oklahoma, and had approximately five years left on my sentence. I remember having a vision. In my vision, I was in a courtroom, and the judge slammed the gavel down and said, "Ninety days." I immediately awakened out of the vision and told my roommate Kory Ellis, "I will be home in ninety days." He said, "Praise the Lord."

Continuing on, I began to tell others about my vision. How many of you know that you can't tell everyone your vision? They began to laugh and talk behind my back. They would say that God did not tell me that. I'm not talking about the people in the world; I am talking about the Christians. "And no marvel, for Satan himself is transformed into an angel of light" (2 Cor 11:14). People will begin to hate you because of your dream. "And Joseph dreamed a dream, and he told it to his brethren, and they hated him yet the more" (Gne 37:5). There is nothing new under the sun; there were haters in 2000 BC, and there are haters today. In Romans l:30, the apostle Paul called them "haters of God."

However, I went to see the parole board, and they told me I was definitely not going to be released. I asked the parole representative, "Are you sure I'm not going to be released?" He stated that he was sure. I then had to go back and face a crowd of critics and naysayers who were waiting to taunt me. They asked, "Well, are you going home?" I stated, "Not yet, but I believe God, and it's not over until God says it's over!"

I remember walking back in that cell and wanting to just get in the bed and put my head under the covers. The enemy came and tried to discourage me from believing in the vision. I was scheduled to preach prior to me seeing the parole board. The message I believed God had given me to preach, even before the vision, was "It's not over until God says it's over." I knew I was living out the very message I had prepared to preach. I was actually living the message out in my life.

I began to stand on the word that God had given me. I called home and told my mother I will be home in ninety days. I began to tell everyone I will be home in ninety days. I made up in my mind that I was going to preach that message with everything I had within me. I remember walking back and forth in front of that church, preaching to the inmates and visitors that it's not over until God says it's over.

To make a long story short, my uncle called the parole chairman who oversees the Department of Corrections. Parole Chairman Leonard Wells, who works in Madison, the state's capital, drove to go sit with my parents in Milwaukee. He assured them that I would be coming home. Subsequently, I was given another hearing, and the representative treated me with preferential treatment. He said, "We are getting you ready to be home in ninety days." I'm here to tell you, if it is a God-given vision, He will bring it to pass. Don't worry about the naysayers, don't worry about your critics, and don't worry about the haters.

It's not over until God says it's over.

The Devil Prompts Us to Fulfill the Vision in Our Own Strength

Whenever we try to fulfill the vision in our own strength, without God, it results in conflicts. God had given Abraham a vision that he would be the father of many nations. However, Abraham tried to fulfill this by having a baby (Ishmael) by Sarah's handmaid, instead of waiting for God to bring the promise to pass.

I once heard a story that a preacher told about a man whose gas had been turned off. He said the man tried to resolve the problem by tapping into his neighbor's gas line, and ended up blowing up both houses. We have to trust God to bring the promise to pass. I also heard a preacher say that some women look for men who are strong and muscular like Tarzan. He went on to say that not only did one woman get Tarzan, but he also had a little Jane and a cheetah (crazy, wild) inside of him too. We have to learn to wait for God. We can't let our biological clocks rush us into choosing the wrong partner.

We Don't Have to Help God, He Is Our Very Present Help

There is no need for us to feel that we have to help God. Interestingly, the Bible tells the story of the Philistines and their god Dagon. The name Dagon is derived from *dag*, meaning "a fish." The fish was symbolic of its reproductive powers, since some fish have been known to lay as many as thirty million eggs annually. Some theologians have said that Dagon resembled a mermaid—half-fish and half-man. The Bible says: "When the Philistines took the ark of God, they brought it into the hose of Dagon, and set it by Dagon. And when Ashdod arose early in the morning, behold,

Dagon was fallen upon his face to the earth before the ark of the Lord. And they took Dagon and set him in his place again. (1 Sm 5:2–3).

The Philistines had to help their god. What kind of god would you have to set back in his place? What kind of God would you have to help back up? I thank God that I serve a God that doesn't need my assistance, He doesn't need my help. "God is our strength, a very present help in the time of trouble" (Ps 46:1). If you have a hard time believing this, pray, "Lord I believe; help thou my unbelief" (Mk 9:24). The psalmist said: "I will lift mine eyes unto the hills, from whence cometh my help. My help cometh from the Lord, which made heaven and earth" (Ps 121:1–2).

God Is Up To Something

"And He said, 'Go forth, and stand upon the mount before the Lord. And behold, the Lord passed by, and a great, strong wind rent the mountains and broke in pieces the rocks before the Lord, but the Lord was not in the wind. And after the wind an earthquake, but the Lord was not in the earthquake. And after the earthquake a fire, but the Lord was not in the fire. And after the fire a still small voice" (1 Kgs 19:11–12).

If you have any children or have ever observed children, you probably know that as long as they are playing and making noise, they are okay. But as soon as there is silence, and they are quiet, you immediately know that they are up to something. If it seems as though God is quiet in your life, don't worry, don't become dismayed. He's up to something!

We Should Never Give Up

Robin Roberts of *Good Morning America* interviewed sixty-four-year old Diana Nyad. This sixty-four-year-old woman successfully swam 110 miles from Cuba to Florida on her fifth attempt. She battled rough seas, sharks, and the world's most deadly jellyfish. She had no protective shark cage. She arrived to shore some fifty-three hours later badly sunburned, and with a swollen tongue and lips from swallowing saltwater for days. She said she was looking for a television camera, and when she spotted one, she said, "We should never give up!" Diana Nyad went on to say, "You're never too old to chase your dreams."

Amazingly, before I could even finish writing this chapter, I saw this lady on the news again. This time they said that she swam forty-eight straight hours in a swimming pool without taking a break, in efforts to raise money for the survivors of Superstorm Sandy.

Chapter 5

AGAINST ALL ODDS

The foundation of high school and college statistic courses is the introduction of the probability theory. The probability theory is simply the study of statistics, averages, chance, and odds. Oftentimes when we are watching the weather forecast, we note that the weatherman sometimes states that there could be a 70 percent chance of rain. Some forecasts also state that there is a chance or that it is likely that it will rain. The Gallup poll conducts a thousand interviews a day, 360 days a year, to gather statistics for their polls. We live in a society that has become inundated with percentages, averages, and odds.

Chances are, if you are like me, at some point in your life, you have defied the odds. The doctors may have said that you wouldn't make it this far, but you are reading this book right now because against all odds, you are still here. You've heard that 50 percent of all marriages end in divorce, but you're still married. People have told you that you would never be anything, or never amount to nothing, but against all odds, you have prevailed against your critics. "If God be for us, who can be against us?" (Rom 8:31). We serve a God that goes against all reason, against all logic, and against all odds.

On a spring evening in May 1998, Donald Staley was in a violent tornado in Moore, Oklahoma. The tornado was very destructive, peeling off his roof. The following spring of May 1999, an F5, the single most vicious tornado, hit Oklahoma again and ruined some eight thousand homes. Donald Staley's home was hit again while he took shelter in the bathtub with his pets. Unluckily, some four years later, on May 3, 2003, yet another tornado demolished his home. Against all odds, he survived three catastrophic storms, where the death tolls and injured were in the thousands. The *New York Times* quoted someone stating, "You go to look for the street, but the whole street is gone. Sometimes you go to look, and the whole neighborhood is gone."

While the chances of being hit twice by tornados in two consecutive years is about one in a million, the chances of being hit by three tornados in six years is about one in three trillion. Against all odds, he survived all three tornadoes and found out firsthand that God will literally be your shelter in the time of storms. Amazingly, after the storm, he was flooded with news media interviews and went on to appear in a television commercial advertising the storm shelter that saved his life. Likewise, we have been through the storms in our lives, where the chances of surviving were nil to none, but against all odds, we're still here to tell the story. Like Mr. Staley, we need to tell others about the shelter in the midst of the storm that saved our lives.

Not to mention, 112 out of 115 polls predicted Hillary Clinton would win the presidential election. Some political analysts predicted Hillary had as much as a 95 to 96 percent chance of becoming president. In spite of the odds, Donald Trump won the election in a stunning upset, and became the first president in history without any political or military experience. "Surreal" was the most searched word during the year Trump was elected president. The largest spike in the use of the word "surreal "was after the presidential election

Defying the Odds

More than one hundred thousand people enter US prisons and jails each week, according to the Bureau of Justice statistics. In addition, one in thirty-five Americans in some way is caught up in the criminal justice system. For decades, the United States has had the world's largest prison population by far.

Countless incarcerated men and women throughout history have continuously defied the odds and boundaries society has placed on them. They have refused to become a statistic. Eleanor Roosevelt stated, "Nobody can make you feel inferior without your consent." Remarkably, prisoners have gone on to accomplish great feats. Prisoners have won the Nobel Peace Prize, made great contributions to advances in medicine, science, and inventions that have helped literally shape the awesome landscape of the world we live in.

Namely, while locked up, Jesse Hawley developed the plans for the Erie Canal. Not to mention, America, with all its valor, would not have won World War II, if it had not been for a prisoner and gunsmith named David Marshall Williams.

Miraculously, a prisoner named Paul defied the odds, and penned inspiring and instructional "prison epistles," writing about two-thirds of the New Testament from a jail cell. An inmate named Miguel de Cervantes wrote the first modern novel. Moreover, a convict by the name of William Addis invented the first mass-produced toothbrush from the big house. Surprisingly, a jailbird named Robert Stroud discovered a cure for septicemia (blood poisoning) and went on to become a much-respected *ornithologist* (bird studier). He was also known as the Birdman of Alcatraz.

Rebound

Michael Jordan had everything—three championships, gold medals, notoriety, and fame. But when tragedy struck, he chose to go to the sidelines to rebound. More importantly, he was able to bounce back, pack sold-out arenas, and win three more championships. Likewise, you have to make up your mind and say, "I am going to defy the odds." You have to rebound and refuse to rebound; refuse to succumb to the negative stigma that society and your haters have placed on you. There is an American proverb that says, "Doubt whom you will, but never doubt yourself." The Honorable Judge Mathis stated, "A lot of people have criminal records, me included." As a matter of fact, numerous people have been released from jails and prisons all over the world, and have gone on to have successful careers, such as Judge Mathis, and countless people less known.

Incredibly, just five years after being released from prison, Martha Stewart defied the odds, rebounded, and employed some six hundred people, added seven thousand new products to her name, ran four magazines, and published her seventy-first book. She also had four television shows on the Hallmark Channel. While the names have all changed, the game is still the same. You have got to rebound, get back up, defy the odds, and get back in the game of life.

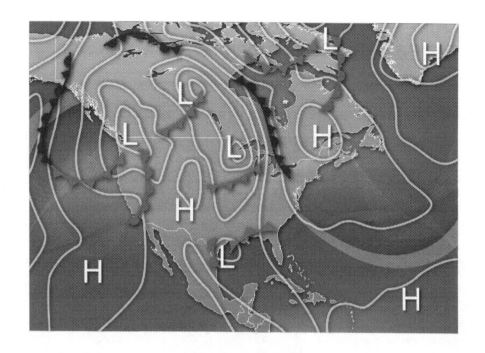

Chapter 6

HIGHS AND LOWS

M any meteorologists forecast the weather using highs and lows. For example, they may say, "Mostly cloudy with a chance of scattered storms. Highs, mid-seventies, and lows in the mid-forties." Some may even give you a record high or low for that particular day. High pressure systems are typically associated with fair weather conditions, while low pressure systems usually bring cloudy skies and precipitation. We also experience record highs and lows in our lives.

If you have ever seen an electrocardiograph machine (a device used for recording the mechanical movements of the heart), you've noticed that once the electrodes are attached to the patient's body, the electrocardiograph moves up and down, resembling life. Each time the heart beats, it produces electric currents, signified by high and low lines on the ECG. The moment the electrocardiograph stops going up and down and shows a horizontal line, it is indicating no life or a flat-line. The fact that you are experiencing highs and lows in life is just the reality that you are still living.

Matt Lauer was interviewing Olympic gold medalist Miss Franklin on the *Today* show. He stated, "You deal with the highs and lows." Comparatively, he also told her, "You dealt with the highs of winning in London, and the lows of a Rio disappointment." Additionally, she was promoting her new book, *Relentless Spirit*. Similarly, we also have to have a relentless spirit to deal with the highs and lows.

When They Go Low, We Go High

First Lady Michelle Obama delivered a powerful speech at the Democratic National Convention. The *New York Times* noted, "OK, Michelle Obama stole the show." The *New York Daily News* even scrapped their original plan for the paper's front page. Their new headline read, "Michelle's Speech Brings Down the House."

The first lady went on to elaborate, "That is the story of this country. The story that has brought me to this stage tonight. The stories of generations of people who felt the lash of bondage, the shame of servitude, the sting of segregation, but who kept striving and hoping and doing what is needed to be done so that today, I wake up every morning in a house that was built by slaves."

The first lady talked about lessons that she and the president try to teach their daughters. "How we explain when someone is cruel or act like a bully, you don't stoop to their level. No, our motto is: 'When they go low, we go high.'" Despite their critics, they rose to become the most powerful couple in the world. Regardless of those that took the low road, Obama was elected president of the United States. Always remember, when your critics, naysayers, enemies, and haters take the low road, maintain your integrity and take the high road. "The Lord said to my Lord, 'Sit at My right hand, till I make your enemies your footstool'" (Ps).

God has not promised us sunshine, but a little rain mixed with sunshine so we can appreciate the good times. Be grateful. I know it's hard while you're going through it, but remember, seasons must change.

The Bible tells the story of Israel, who defeated their enemies in the hills. The enemies of Israel stated, "Their gods are gods of the hills, therefore they were stronger than we, but let us fight them in the plain [valley], and surely we shall be stronger than they" (1 Kgs 20:23 Amplified Bible). Their rationale was that Israel only served a God that could help them in the hills, and not in the valleys.

"And there came a man of God, and spake unto the king of Israel and said, 'Thus saith the Lord, because the Syrians have said the Lord is God of the hills, but He is not God of the valleys. Therefore will I deliver all this great multitude into thine hand, and ye shall know that I am the Lord" (1 Kgs 20:28).

Essentially, what God is saying is that despite your enemies saying that He is only a God of the hills (high points of your life), and not a God of the valleys (your lows and depressions), He will deliver you, and you shall know that He is God. A valley is elongated lowland between hills or mountains. There are going to be some mountaintop experiences in our lives, as well as valley-low experiences.

450 to 1

The Bible tells the story of Gideon, who went up to fight against an army of 135,000 troops. Gideon started out with thirty-two thousand men, but God reduced the number to just a measly three hundred, so others would know that it was God who delivered them and not them themselves. By all accounts, the odds were 450 to 1, in favor of the Midianites (enemy). However, the Word of God says, "A thousand shall fall at thy side and ten thousand at thy right hand, but it shall not come nigh thee" (Ps 91:7).

God allows the odds to mount up against us, to the point where we have no choice but to call upon Him. It is during these times of weakness that God lets us know, "My grace is sufficient for thee, for my strength is made perfect in weakness" (2 Cor 12:9). Despite the odds, despite Gideon's enemies and weaknesses, God considered him a "mighty man of valor" (Judg 6:12).

We serve a God that likes to get the glory out of our situation, and He has stated, "I will not give my glory to another" (Is 48:11). Therefore, God takes pleasure in lifting up those that society has counted out.

Sorry, Wrong Number

The problem with probability theory (statistics, chance, and odds) is that their guidelines for interpreting numbers can be biased. Some numbers are pretty good, while many are not. For example, if you take a select group of individuals and say that their annual average income is $40,000, that number significantly changes if one of those individuals happens to be multibillionaire Warren Buffet.

In contrast, statistical literacy teaches you how to look critically at statistics and numbers. If someone tries to add up the failures of your past, let them know your calculations are wrong. Tell them to go figure, sorry, wrong number.

My facilitator called me into her office and performed what is called a compass test. A compass test gathers together all the data about you and your past and assesses the probability of you returning to prison based on percentages. To my dismay, I was told that there was an 85 percent chance of me returning to prison, based on this test.

I certainly didn't receive the results of that test, because I knew that there was a 100 percent chance that I will return to prison, but not as the test predicted. I would return as a visitor to encourage others.

In the midst of the storm, even as I write, I can see myself telling others that my facilitator had the wrong number. They said at the rate I was going, I wouldn't live to see the age of eighteen, but they had the wrong number. Whose report shall we believe? We shall believe the report of the Lord. You are not a statistic. Against all odds, you are still here.

Chapter 7

STORM CHASERS

Man-Made Storms

The sea of Galilee sets the topography of what would become a historic, life-changing adventure at sea. This lake is positioned some several hundred feet below sea level, and is surrounded by mountainous peaks that rise three to four thousand feet above sea level. The combination of warm tropical air, coupled with colder air from the nearby hills, creates a turbulence that can produce great swells and waves—or, in essence, the perfect storm. We read:

"And the same day, when the evening was come, he saith unto them, 'Let us pass over to the other side.' And when they had sent away the multitude, they took him even as he was in the ship. And there arose a great storm of wind, and the waves beat into the ship, so that it was now full. And he arose and rebuked the wind, and said to the sea, 'Peace, be still.' And the wind ceased, and there was a great calm. And he said unto them, 'Why are you so fearful? How is it you have no faith?' And they feared exceedingly, and said one to another, 'What manner of man is this, that even the wind and sea obey him?'" (Mk 4:35–41).

The National Weather Service issues warnings of impending threats or danger. While most people run for cover when the siren sounds, some enthusiasts chase these violent and catastrophic storms. Discovery Channel premiered a series called *Storm Chasers*. These radical storm chasers drive their outfitted vehicles equipped with meteorological instrumentation at speeds of over 100 miles per hour into category EF3 and EF4 storms. These storms have recorded wind speeds of over 175 miles per hour. The Internet, digital cameras, and smart phones have created an explosion of amateur storm chasers.

The Gospel of Mark, chapter four, gives us an eyewitness account of what would become a story of epic proportions. Jesus begins by teaching lessons on the sea. Later that evening, He gives His disciples a courageous invitation to get in the boats and "go over to the other side." The disciples knew this was a daring feat because on the "other side" were pagans, heathens, demons, and unclean spirits. How many of you reading this right now know that the grass is not always greener on the "other side"?

I have ended a relationship, thought I was moving on to something better, and found out that the grass was not greener on the "other side."

Peradventure, the crew set sail and there "arose a great storm" of biblical proportions. Samuel Johnson stated, "Going to sea is going to prison, with a chance at drowning besides." I can only imagine that as they took part in this wild ride, that they looked at the ominous, marbled grey sea surrounded by dark mountains, and then looked to Jesus. "This hope is like a firm and steady anchor for our souls" (Heb 6:19 CEV).

Quickly, the breaking waves began to vehemently "beat into the ship," causing the sheer force of water to pour into the boat, "so that it was now full." They were fearful of being buried at sea—there were no coast guards, rescue helicopters. They began bailing water out of the boat to keep from drowning, just as fast as it was coming in. By the same token, in life, it seems just as fast as we get bailed out of one problem, we are faced with a tidal wave of trouble.

Interestingly, naval architects perform stress tests on ships to determine the level of stress the ship is likely to encounter during a lifetime. However, there are ships that come face-to-face with waves that far exceed their stress ratings. Naval architects call the waves "nonnegotiable waves." Being a certified credit counselor, the term "nonnegotiable" caught my undivided attention. I have often called to negotiate payments for my clients. However, when the "nonnegotiable waves" of life are rising, it seems as though as soon as we get bailed out on the water bill, we are up to our necks in other debts.

Let's Cut Right to the Chase

Some storm chasers chase storms for profit, and make up to five figures selling pictures of awesome-looking storms, and other storm chasers use "nonnegotiable" instruments (fraudulent) as a means of making illegal money. On the other hand, some storm chasers chase storms for the adrenaline rush and excitement. Some companies even offer storm chasing tours. You can pay a fee and take the ride of your life as a "storm tourist," chasing a dangerous, life-threatening storm. I will be the first to say I am guilty of chasing storms. When I was younger, I was in a high-speed chase. I was dangerously accelerating at speeds of over 100 miles per hour through red lights, intersections, and stop signs on the city streets, being airborne at times. Even as I write, I thank God that no pedestrians or cars were crossing those intersections and that miraculously, no one got injured. After the chase, they stated, "Is the car stolen?" I stated, "No." They stated, "Why were you running then?" As I look back now, I was a storm chaser, and I was chasing a storm.

In the midst of the storm, Jesus said, "'Peace, be still!' And the wind ceased, and there was a great calm" (Mk 4:39). All of a sudden, "they were terrified and asked each other, 'Who is this? Even the wind and the waves obey him!'" (Mk 4:41 NIV). The point is that they were more "terrified" of the peace than being in the actual storm. Likewise, some people aren't happy unless they have something to worry about.

In the storm, we pray fast and get in the face of God, but after the storm, we stop doing the very things that got us out in the first place. I know a person who was in jail and prayed to get out. He got out and came back to the exact same cell some time later.

Can we stand to be blessed?

For example, I was blessed with the newest Mercedes Benz truck on the market and found myself driving past the church and chasing drugs and women. On the contrary, whatever we did to get through the storm is the same thing we have to do to keep from chasing the next storm. The same things (praying, sowing, worshiping) we did in the midst of the storm are exactly the same things we need to continue doing after the storm is over.

The boat set shore, and "they came to the other side of the sea, and encountered Legion. Jesus ultimately cast out thousands of evil spirits, teaching the disciples that 'one man shall "chase" a thousand, for the Lord your God, he is that fiteth for you'" (Jo 23:10).

Chapter 8

Pray in the Midst of the Storm

Prayer Changes Things

I can remember being forced to drive a car with a gun pressed up against my neck, while another person kept an eye on me from the backseat. I can still remember the feeling of the cold steel as I drove across town. I began to pray in the Spirit, and the gunmen began to laugh. Jude 20 says, "But ye, beloved, building up yourselves on your most holy faith, praying in the Holy Ghost."

I finally arrived in a house on the north side of Milwaukee, and was ordered out of the car at gunpoint. As I arrived in the house, there was a room with vicious pit bull dogs in it. I looked in the room, and the windows were boarded up. I could hear someone say, "Put him in the room with the dogs." They decided not to put me in the room with the dogs, but to shoot me instead. One of the men told the other one to turn the stereo up loud in an attempt to drown out the sound of the gunshots.

All of a sudden, I was directed toward the basement. As I began to go down the basement stairs, he realized that there were no lights on down there, so he stopped me on a stair landing. He pointed the gun at me and demanded that I back up into the corner. I said, "I know you are going to shoot me, but just let me pray first." He stated, "Ain't no sense in praying now." Realizing that all hope was lost, and that I had nothing to lose, I got down on my knees and began to pray in the Spirit. The Word teaches:

Likewise, the Spirit also helps our infirmities, for we know not what we should pray for as we ought, but the spirit itself makes intercession for us with groaning which cannot be uttered.

"And he that searcheth the hearts knoweth what is the mind of the Spirit, because he maketh intercession for the saints according to the will of God" (Rom 8:26–27).

While on my knees praying, I jumped up and grabbed the gun. We began to wrestle and struggle over the gun, and I heard a loud gunshot ring in my ears, and saw fire from the bullet as hit the brick wall. I was holding on to the gun for dear life when the other gunman came and put a different gun to my head and said, "Let the gun go." I knew I had messed up and it was over for me. The other man went back to watch out so the other one could shoot me, and before I knew it, I grabbed the gun again. Even though he was much larger than I was, I wrestled my way up the stairs and ended up jumping through a glass window to hasten my escape. I must inform you that this person was notoriously known for robbing drug dealers, and had already been to jail for murder. Yet I'm here writing this book and lived to tell this story because prayer changes things.

Make It Rain

There is a new trend that is taking our society by storm. It is called "making it rain." The object is to show others that essentially, you got it going on. This is done by taking an extremely large stack of money and causing it to go up into the air one bill at a time and come down, thus making it rain. The person usually walks off and lets the less fortunate pick up the cash. While this has become a craze in twenty-first century, in biblical times, Elijah literally made it rain.

Elijah was a human being with a nature such as we have (with feelings, affections, and a constitution like ours). He prayed earnestly for it not to rain, and no rain fell on the earth for three years and six months (1 Kgs 17:1).

"And [then] he prayed again, and the heavens supplied rain, and the land produced its crops [as usual]" (James 5:17 Amplified Bible).

The Bible says, "Elijah was a prophet from Tishbe in Gilead. One day he went to King Ahab and said, 'I'm a servant of the living Lord, the God of Israel. And I swear in his name that it won't rain until I say so. There won't even be any dew on the ground'" (1 Kgs 17:1 CEV). Elijah prayed, and "a few minutes later, it got very cloudy and windy, and rain started pouring down" (1 Kgs 18:45 CEV).

Elijah was just a person like we are, yet he made it rain. I have heard of accounts where farmers have actually prayed for rain, and it miraculously fell from the sky. While some may not believe the many documented accounts of the miracles God has performed, one thing is certain, and that is that prayer changes things.

Partner-Ship (Two Partners in a Ship)

Partnership has played a vital role in the numerous victories I have experienced over the years. I have partnered with many ministries, and have also supported them financially. Some of my partners have committed to praying for me and my family on a daily basis. This promise is so powerful: "I promise that when any two of you on earth agree about something you are praying for, my Father in heaven will do it for you" (Mt 18:19 CEV).

The Bible tells the story of how David and his men went out to battle. "David led his six hundred men to Besor George, but two hundred of them were too tired to go across. So they stayed behind, while David and the other four hundred men crossed the gorge" (1 Sm 30:10). He started out with six hundred men, and about ten to twenty miles later, he had plainly four hundred because "two hundred abode behind, which were so faint that they could not go over the brook Besor" (1 Sm 30:10).

The Bible lets us know that eventually David conquered his enemies, "and David smote them from the twilight even unto the evening of the next day . . . And David recovered all . . . And David took all the flocks and the herds, which the drove before those other cattle, and said, 'This is David's spoil'" (1 Sm 30:17–20).

Then David goes on to give us a biblical illustration of partnership. When David and his four hundred men came back to the two hundred that were too tired to go to battle, some of David's men were good-for-nothings, and they said, "Those men didn't go with us to battle, so they don't get any of the things we took" (1 Sm 30:22 CEV). "Then said David, 'Ye shall not do so, my brethren, with that which the Lord hath given us, and delivered the company that came against us into our hand. For who will hearken unto you in this matter? But as his part is that goeth down to the battle, so shall his part be that tarrieth by the stuff: they shall be alike'" (1 Sm 30:24).

David understood the importance of partnership and made it a law throughout all Israel. He told the others regardless if others didn't take part in the actual fighting, it's share and share alike. While I have not been to the many countries where my partners are preaching the gospel, I have supported my partners financially. Therefore, I have reaped the benefits and rewards of their efforts.

In fact, while I was writing this book, the Americans won the American Cup. This a boat race where the crew consists of eleven of the most accomplished sailors in the world. Miraculously, the Americans came back from an eight to one deficit against New Zealand. The sports commentators said that this type of comeback had never before been done in history. Interestingly, the name of the Americans' boat was the *Oracle*.

In Hebrew, one of the words for the word oracle is *debyr,* meaning "the innermost part of the sanctuary." When you partner with others, and enter the innermost part of the sanctuary, you will experience miracles in your life as well. I heard someone say that partnership was just two partners in a ship.

We may not have all come over in the same ship, but we're all in the same boat. If we will partner with other ministries and individuals that are doing the work of the Lord, we will reap the benefits and share in the anointing that are on our partners.

Prayer of Agreement

The prayer of agreement is another prayer that has been essential in my personal prayer life. Matthew 18:19 says, "Again I say unto you, that if two of you shall agree on earth as touching anything that they shall ask, it shall be done for them of my father which is in heaven." The word "agree" in this text is *sumphoneo* in Greek, which means "to be harmonious." It is where we get the word "symphony." To be harmonious with someone in prayer, you have to be on one accord.

Discord

In contrast, association brings on assimilation; we can't come into agreement with everyone, because everyone doesn't believe that God is able to do the impossible. "And it is no wonder. Even Satan tries to make himself look like an angel of light. So why does it seem strange for Satan's servants to pretend to do what is right?" (2 Cor 11:14–15 CEV). Solomon, in his wisdom, stated, "Those crooks will disappear when the storm strikes, but God will keep safe all who obey Him" (Prv 10:25 CEV*).* The prayer of agreement is a powerful weapon in the warfare of prayer. The Word of God asks, "Can two people walk together without agreeing to meet?" (Am 3:3 CEV).

Don't Waver in the Storm

If any of you are deficient in wisdom, let him ask of the giving God, who gives to everyone liberally and ungrudgingly, without reproaching or faultfinding, and it will be given him.

Only it must be in faith that he asks with no wavering (no hesitating, no doubting). For the one who wavers is like the billowing surge out at sea that is blown hither and thither and tossed by the wind. For truly, let not such a person imagine that he will receive anything he asks for from the

Lord, "[being as he is] a man of two minds (hesitating, dubious, irresolute), and uncertain about everything [he thinks, feels, decides]" (Jas 1:5–8 Amplified Bible).

James 1:8 says "A double-minded man is unstable in all his ways." The word "double-minded" is only used in this Scripture. The term literally means "of two minds or souls." One Bible version (HCSB) calls the person an "indecisive man." Many times we ask God for something and resort right back to our own wisdom. First Kings 18:21 in the Amplified Bible says, "How long will you halt and limp between two opinions?"

We have to come to a point in our prayer life where we learn to trust in God. It takes the same amount of energy to worry about a problem as it does to pray about it. I know it is easier said than done, but when we put a problem in God's hands, we have to leave it there. When the devil comes and tries to discourage you, let him know he's talking to the wrong person, because you gave that problem to God.

We can learn from the life of Abraham, notably how "no unbelief or distrust made him waver (doubtingly question) concerning the promises of God, but he grew strong and was empowered by faith as he gave praise and glory to God" (Rom 4:20 Amplified Bible).

Prayer Scriptures

I thank God for praying grandmothers. James explained this truth: "The effectual fervent prayer of a righteous man [or woman] availeth much" (Jas 5: 16, emphasis added).

And this is the confidence (the assurance, the privilege of boldness) which we have in Him: we are sure that if we ask anything (make any request) according to His will (in agreement with His own plan), He listens and hears us. And if we positively know that He listens to us in whatever we ask, we also know—with settled, absolute knowledge—that we have granted us as our present possessions the request made of Him" (1 Jn 5:14–15).

"Whenever you stand up to pray, you must forgive what others have done to you. Then your father in heaven will forgive your sins" (Mk 11:25–26).

"If you have faith in God and don't doubt His heart, you can tell this mountain to get up and jump into the sea, and it will. Everything you ask for in prayer will be yours, if you only have faith" (Mark 11:23–24).

"I will answer their prayers before they finish praying" (Is 65:24 CEV).

Forgiveness

If we freely admit that we have sinned and confess our sins, He is faithful and just (true to His own nature and promises) and will forgive our sins, dismiss our lawlessness, and continually cleanse us from all unrighteousness—everything not in conformity to His will, purpose, thought, and action (1 Jn 1:9 Amplified Bible).

"As far as the east is from the west, so far has He removed our transgressions from us" (Ps 103:12).

"Beloved, never avenge yourselves, but leave the way open for [God's] wrath; for it is written, 'Vengeance is Mine, I will repay [requite],' says the Lord" (Rom 12:19 Amplified Bible).

Jesus taught His disciples to pray "and forgive us our debts as we also have forgiven [left remitted], and let go of the debts, and have given up resentment against] our debtors (Mt 6:12 Amplified Bible).

Whenever you stand up to pray, you must forgive what others have done to you. Then your Father in heaven will forgive your sins (Mk 11:25–26 CEV).

Prayer for Favor

In the name of Jesus, [your name or family name here] is the righteousness of God, therefore [I or we] are entitled to covenant love, kindness, and favor.

The favor of God is among and surrounds the righteous, therefore it surrounds [your name or family name here] everywhere they go. And in everything that [your name or family name here] [we or I do], I expect the favor of God to be in manifestation.

Never again will I be without the favor of God; it rests richly upon me and profusely abounds in me. I am part of the generation that is experiencing it immeasurably, limitlessly, and surpassingly.

Therefore, favor produces promotion, restoration, honor, prominence, supernatural increase, increased assets, greater victories, preferential treatment, petitions granted, policies and rules changed, and battles won, which [I or we] do not have to fight.

This is the year and day of God's favor in [your name or family name here]'s life; therefore [name here]'s life will never be the same, in Jesus's name.

Chapter 9

SOW IN THE MIDST OF THE STORM

Torrential financial storms flooded throughout the economy as the real estate bubble burst. The stock market crashed, and unemployment spiraled out of control. Homeowners were drowning in debt and under floodwater with their mortgages. Interest rates were exorbitant, and consumer confidence was down. America's working class was now America's homeless. Congress voted on bailing out lending institutions, automakers, and the world's largest banks, including Wells Fargo, Chase, and Bank of America. Countless people lined up to receive food from the Red Cross, United Way, Salvation Army, and church pantries all around the world.

This was the worst recession since the 1930s Great Depression. We were experiencing economic contractions, and America was in a famine of biblical proportions.

Many people throughout history have suffered or died of starvation when food was scarce, or crops failed. There have also been documented famines during wars. About nine million Chinese people died as the result of a famine, and in 1837, a famine in India killed about eight hundred thousand as a result of food shortage.

"And there was a famine [storm] in the land, besides the first famine [storm] that was in the days of Abraham . . . Then Isaac sowed in that land [storm] and received in the same year a hundredfold. And the Lord blessed him" (Gn 26:1,12, emphasis mine).

Peradventure, the Bible tells the story of Isaac who was faced with a far worse situation than we were faced with in the Great Recession (2007 to 2011). He was literally surrounded by utter famine and starvation. The famine had no boundaries and crossed all ethnic barriers. Everyone was starving, even the king. However, in the midst of the storm, Isaac made a conscious decision to step out in faith and sow in a barren land. Isaac understood that he didn't have to wait for the conditions to become favorable to sow

We learn that Isaac "became rich, and his wealth continued to grow until he became very wealthy" (Gn 26:13). With Isaac gaining wealth came the haters also. "Isaac said unto them, 'Wherefore come to me, seeing ye hate me.'" They saw how the Lord was blessing him as a result of him sowing in the storm. They stated, "We saw clearly that the Lord was with you." As you begin to sow in the midst of the storm, don't be surprised of the hate toward you, while others try to get close to you.

Many people take on different challenges. There was a fad going around called the mannequin challenge. It went viral all the way to the White House. People everywhere were imitating mannequins. There was another one called the water bottle challenge, where even NBA players attempted to flip a water bottle and make it land on the bottom. Additionally, every New Year, millions of people make a New Year's resolution. In fact, there is a challenge in the Scripture where God says, "Try it! Put me to the test!" (Mal 3:10) in regards to tithes.

We read: "'Bring all the tithes [the whole tenth of your income] into the storehouse, that there may be found food in My house, and prove Me by it,' says the Lord of hosts. 'If I will not open the windows of heaven for you and pour you out a blessing, that there shall not be room enough to receive it' (Malachi 2:2, 3:8–10 Amplified Bible).

Please note that I struggled greatly with adding this section to this book because I knew that I would have to expose my giving to others. Nevertheless, I came to the conclusion that I would be doing my readers a great disservice if I didn't include this essential principle, "sowing in the storm."

Continuing on, I personally made up my mind that I was going step out in faith and begin to sow in the storm (prison). Note that this was a big step for me because prison wages only amount to approximately $20 per month in Wisconsin. My first goal was to sow $3 into a ministry with worldwide missions (sow in good ground).

My next goal was $7. I knew that the number seven was significant in the Bible and was the number of completion. So I sowed, believing that God would complete some things in my life. I graduated to $8 because there were eight people on the ark, and it symbolized a new beginning. If anyone needed a new beginning, it certainly was me. As I began to sow, God began to give me seed. He gives seed to the sower. To make a long story short, I was able to sow seventy, several hundred, and ultimately thousands, into churches, and missions around the world—all from a prison cell. As I began to sow, I began to reap supernatural blessing, financially and spiritually. God began to provide health, favor, healing, and divine protection for me and my family.

In sum, regardless of how grim the situation was, Isaac held on to the promise, "I will be with thee, and I will bless thee." Sow in the midst of the storm, and believe in a supernatural God to multiply your natural seed. You can also sow with your time. Donate your time to helping others, and watch God help you. "Give, and it shall be given unto you; pressed down, and shaken together, and running over shall men give unto your bosom" (Lk 6:38).

Chapter 10

STANDING ON THE WORD IN THE MIDST OF THE STORM

There are 783,000 words in the Bible, approximately 3,573 promises, and there comes a time in our lives where we will be required to stand on the Word. I speak from experience. There was a time in my life where I took the Bible and set it on the floor and literally stood on top of it. I told God, "I am standing on your Word. It doesn't matter what it looks like, I'm not worried about the circumstances. I'm standing on your Word. You said, 'For out of prison, he cometh to reign'" (Eccl 4:14). You said that you would open doors that no man can close" (Is 61:3). The Bible says, "and having done all to stand, stand." We have to make up in our minds that we will stand on the Word. In the book of Isaiah, He says, "Put Me in remembrance [of my Word]" (Is 43:26, emphasis mine).

In fact, God says, "Heaven and earth shall pass away, but my words shall not pass away" (Mt 24:35). We have to come to a position, even in the midst of the storm, where we make a declaration to stand on the Word. "For the word of God is quick and powerful, and sharper than any two-edged sword, piercing even to the dividing asunder of soul and spirit, and joints and marrow, and is a discerner of the thoughts and intents of the heart" (Heb 4:12).

The following is an illustration of standing on the Word in an actual storm:

"But the ship was now in the midst of the sea, tossed with waves, for the wind was contrary. And in the fourth watch of the night, Jesus went unto them, walking on the sea. And when the disciples saw Him walking on the sea, they were troubled, saying, 'It is a spirit,' and they cried out in fear.

"But straightaway Jesus spoke unto them, saying, 'Be of good cheer. It is I, be not afraid.' And Peter answered him and said, 'Lord, if it be thou, bid me come unto thee on the water.' And He said, 'Come.' And when Peter was come down out of the ship, he walked on the water to go to Jesus" (Mt 14:24–29).

On the positive side, Peter was literally able to stand on the Word in the midst of the storm. The word "come" spoken by Jesus allowed him to get out of the boat and walk on water. By standing on the Word, Peter was able to do the impossible. The psalmist said, "Order my steps in thy word" (Ps 119:133). David prayed, "Uphold my steps in your path, that my footsteps may not slip" (Ps 17:5 NIV). The Word declares, "Thy word is a lamp unto my feet, and a light unto my path" (Ps 119:105). There comes a time in our lives where we have to get out of the boat and stand on the Word. The journey of a thousand miles begins with one step. Even as I stand in prison and peck the words you're reading, one letter at a time. Regardless of what it looks like, I'm standing on the Word in the midst of the storm. I see myself autographing this book you're reading. As I sign my name, I'm telling someone to stand on the Word.

To enumerate, the Word of God has to become our very sustenance. We have to begin to feed on the Word. "It is written, man shall not live by bread alone, but by every word that proceeded out of the mouth of God" (Mt 4:4). We have to begin to take the Word in, from when we wake up, all throughout the day, and finally meditating on the Word when we go to sleep. Jeremiah understood this concept. He said, "Thy words were found, and I did eat them" (Jer 15:16). We read, "Jesus said unto them, I am the bread of life: he that cometh to me shall never hunger, and he that believeth in me shall never thirst" (Jn 6:35). As we begin to stand on the Word, faith begins to rise up within us. "Faith cometh by hearing, and hearing the word of God" (Rom 10:17). The more we begin to meditate on the word, the more it will begin to flow out of our mouths. Watch some TBN, Word Network, Daystar, or your favorite teaching CD. "For out of the abundance of the heart, the mouth speaketh" (Lk 6:45).

On the other hand, Peter began to focus on the storm, instead of the Word that allowed him to walk on the water in the first place. "But when he saw that the wind was boisterous, he was afraid;

and beginning to sink, he cried, 'Lord, save me.' And immediately Jesus stretched forth His hand and caught him, and said unto him, 'O thou of little faith, wherefore didst thou doubt?'" (Mt 14:30–31).

In the midst of the storm, we cannot waiver, "for he that wavereth is like a wave of the sea driven with the wind and tossed. For let not that man think that he shall receive anything of the Lord. A double-minded man is unstable in all his ways" (Jas 1:6–8).

"Therefore put on God's complete armor, that you may be able to resist and stand your ground on the evil day [of danger], and, having done all [the crisis demands], to stand [firmly in your place]. Stand therefore [hold your ground], having tightened the belt of truth around your loins and having put on the breastplate of integrity and moral rectitude and right standing with God. And having shod your feet in preparation [to face the enemy with firm-footed stability, the promptness and readiness produced by the good news] of the gospel of peace" (Eph 6:13–15 Amplified Bible).

The Scripture says, "Therefore everyone who hears these words of mine and puts them into practice is like a wise man who built his house on the rock. The rain came down, the streams rose, and the winds blew and beat against that house, yet it did not fall because it had its foundation on the rock."

In sum, our bodies are "earthly houses" (see 2 Cor 5:1), and Jesus is that rock. On Christ, the solid rock, I stand. All other ground sings, and there is power in the Word. "He sent forth his word and delivered them from their destructions" (Ps 107:20). "For as the rain cometh down, and the snow from heaven, and returneth not thither, but watereth the earth . . . So shall my word be that goeth forth out of my mouth. It shall not return unto me void, but shall accomplish that which I please, and it shall prosper into the thing whereto I sent it" (Is 55:10–11). And having done all, stand on the Word in the midst of the storm.

Chapter 11

TROUBLE IN PARADISE

Natural beauty and serenity abound in paradise. Paradise Island has stretches of powdery white sand beaches, lush tropical gardens, and beautiful crystal-clear turquoise waters for as far as the eye can see. Paradise Island also has many world-renowned resorts and intimate hideaways. One can embark on an underwater adventure, explore coral reefs, and swim with dolphins. Paradise is picturesque, tranquil, and has sunshine three hundred days a year.

Although this may be true, amid Hurricane Matthew, airports and ports were closed. Cruise ships were diverted away from the island, and tourists were rushed to hotel ballrooms for safety. Paradise Island braced for the blunt of Hurricane Matthew's wrath. Hurricane Matthew made landfall on the Bahamas, inflicting severe impact across several islands. This category 4 storm brought torrential rain and 140-miles-per-hour winds, leaving the island in watery darkness.

In an instant, our lives can be turned upside down, and we too can experience trouble in paradise. In fact, a couple on their honeymoon on Paradise Island watched in sheer horror as their hotel room walls were torn apart and eventually disappeared. Similarly, after the honeymoon bliss, millions of married couples come to the stark realization that there is trouble in paradise. Many couples simply grow apart, and relationships end in earth-shattering breakups.

Man-Made Storms

Hollywood has the capability of mimicking the conditions of an actual storm. Scientists and researchers also have built costly hurricane simulators that can simulate hurricane-force winds of over 120 miles per hour. These are man-made storms. Similarly, in our lives, some of us make storms. All things considered, it is only fitting that since I'm literally in the thick of writing this book, that I give you a forecast out my own storm window. "Lest that by any means, when I have preached to others, I myself should be a castaway" (1 Cor 9:27). As I look down the winding roads and through the vast stretches of wintery woodlands, there is an unmoved calm, free from the hustle and bustle of the big city. In this Mayberry-like suburban middle-class neighborhood, I can look out at my backyard and see huge trees and wildlife tracks in the snow. At the same time, if I were to sweep around my own front door, I would venture to say that there is trouble in paradise.

In other words, I can't blame all the storms I experienced in life as an act of God. Contrary, even with state-of-the-art security and video surveillance around the perimeter of my house, there is an enemy within. I can identify with Paul: "Instead of doing what I know is right, I do wrong. And so, if I don't do what I know is right, I am no longer the one doing these evil things. The sin that lives in me is what does them . . . What a miserable person I am. Who will rescue me from this body that is doomed to die? Thank God! Jesus will rescue me" (Rom 7:19–20, 24–25 CEV).

I have come to the conclusion that every once in a while, there is going to be trouble in paradise. "And there will be earthquakes in various places, and there will be famines and trouble" (Mk 13:8 NKJV). Although this may be true, "do not worry about tomorrow, for tomorrow will bring worries of its own. Today's trouble is enough for today" (Mt 6:34 NRSV). The Bible teaches us with clarity: "Be anxious for nothing, but in everything by prayer and supplication, with thanksgiving, let your request be made known to God. And the peace of God which surpasses all understanding will guard your hearts and minds through Christ Jesus" (Phil 4:7 NKJV).

And "to him who overcomes, I will give to eat from the Tree of Life which is in the midst of Paradise" (Rv 2:7).

There Is No Place Like Home

In wake of Hurricane Katrina, approximately twenty thousand people took shelter in the Louisiana Superdome. The conditions in the dome were catastrophic. There was a breakdown in hygiene, plumbing, and in the urinals, causing it to smell awful. There were also reports of death, gang activity, violence, and rape, causing the many displaced storm victims to come to the vivid realization that there's no place like home.

Amid Hurricane Matthew, there were landslides and flashfloods, and homes were literally flattened or washed away, resulting in widespread evacuations. Hundreds of thousands were ultimately left homeless around the globe, causing thousands of emergency shelters to be opened. Many of the homeless and displaced were repeating that exact phrase, "There's no place like home."

Correspondingly, every year millions of men and women end up serving time in jails and prisons throughout the United States. With this in mind, it's only fitting that I be honest as I literally write in the midst of the storm and trials. At this point in my life, I have spent one-third of my life behind bars. Even as I write from jail now, with Christmas just days away, I can't help but echo that familiar song, "There's No Place Like Home for the Holidays."

Moreover, according to analysis, the home is the single most important investment an individual will make during the course of their lifetime. Annually, there are over a million foreclosures. During the recession, some have stated that America's homeless was once America's middle class. I'm sure the many homeless and displaced would agree that there's no place like home.

The 1939 film *The Wizard of Oz* has become an icon of American culture. It was nominated for six Academy awards, and was named the most viewed motion picture on television. The narrative starts as a powerful tornado rips the house off the very foundation with Dorothy inside. Dorothy is able to look outside the window at all the chaos as the giant twister is spinning the house around. Eventually the house plummets to the ground, and the adventure begins.

Dorothy ultimately closes her eyes and clicks her red ruby slippers together, repeating, "There's no place like home." However, in the 1978 remake of *The Wiz*, Dorothy (Diana Ross) was told, "Home is in your heart." Some would venture to say, where your heart is, your home will be also. The Word states that out of the abundance of the heart, the mouth speaks.

Peradventure, if we were to follow the yellow brick road, there has been a time in our life, even if but for a moment, or somewhere you didn't particularly want to be, when we too have pondered, "There's no place like home."

Having experienced multiple foreclosures, and holding the court filing in my hand, I couldn't help but think of home sweet home. When I received the foreclosure, I "spread the papers out before the Lord" (Hezekiah 19:14), as did Hezekiah on the floor. I thanked God that he was making room for something greater as I danced on those court filings. As I write this some several years later, I can say that I once owed over $300,000 in mortgage payments, but now I live in a home with no mortgage.

It is only appropriate in my synopsis, since Dorothy is a fictional character, that I give you a classic storybook ending. Although Dorothy set out on a journey to Emerald City to see the great and powerful Wizard of Oz behind the curtain, we learn that "by faith, Abraham . . . waited for the city, whose builder and maker is God" (Heb 11:10). The God I serve is not behind a curtain, but "stretches out the heavens like a curtain" (Ps 104:2).

Furthermore, even as I am writing, statistically someone is packing up what used to be home, rather because of divorce, separation, incarceration, or termination of tenancy. If we ease on down the road, we would know that we have a home in the sky, and the streets are made of gold. "For I consider that the sufferings of this present time are not worthy to be compared with the glory which shall be revealed in us" (Rom 8:18). On that note, somewhere over the rainbow, we have a home in the sky.

Chapter 12

THE PERFECT STORM

Bearing Fruit in the Winter

Moreover, the Word of the Lord came to me, saying, "'Jeremiah, what do you see?' And I said, 'I see the branch of an almond tree [the emblem of alertness and activity, blossoming in the winter]'" (Jer 1:11 Amplified Bible). The almond tree is a small tree, and is a member of the peach family. It has pretty pink and white flowers, with a fruit containing a nut. The God we serve is able to cause us to bear fruit and blossom even in the winter (storm). "Then said the Lord to me, 'You have seen well, for I am alert and active, watching over my word to perform it'" (Jer 1:12).

Many of us think that the conditions in our lives have to be favorable for us to reap a harvest, while many others say, "I'm waiting on my season." Ecclesiastes 11:4 says, "He who observes the wind [and waits for all conditions to be favorable] will not sow, and he who regards the clouds will not reap" (Amplified Bible). Imagine if you looked out your window and saw bright and juicy ripe peaches on the branches of trees in the middle of the winter. The prophet Jeremiah saw such a sight, and immediately after, the Lord said, "I will hasten my word to perform it" (Jer 1:12). I know that sounds crazy, but the book of Isaiah says: "For as the rain cometh down, and the snow from heaven and returneth not thither, but watereth the earth, and maketh it bring forth and bud, that it may give seed to the sower, and bread to the eater. So shall my word be that goeth forth out of my mouth. It shall not return unto me void, but it shall accomplish that which I please, and prosper in the thing whereto I sent it" (Is 55:10–11).

God was letting us know that He will watch over His word to perform it, and that it will not return unto Him void. God will bless you in the midst of the storm. Joseph went from the pit, to prison, to the palace.

Joseph named his second son Ephraim, which means "to be fruitful," and Joseph went on to say, "For God hath caused me to be fruitful in the land of my affliction" (Gn 41:52). The Bible says: "Many are the afflictions of the righteous, but the Lord delivereth him out of them all" (Ps 34:19). Joseph was blessed and bore fruit in the midst of the storm. "And the Lord was with Joseph, and he was a prosperous man, and he was in the house of his master the Egyptian" (Gn 39:2). Joseph was blessed even in prison: "But the Lord was with Joseph, and showed him mercy, and gave him favor in the sight of the keepers of the prison" (Gn 39:21).

God caused Joseph to bear fruit in the winter: "And Pharaoh said unto Joseph, 'See I have set thee over all the land of Egypt.' And Pharaoh took off his ring from his hand, and put it upon Joseph's hand, and arrayed him in vestures of fine linen, and put a gold chain about his neck. And he made him to ride in the second chariot which he had; and they cried before him, 'Bow the knee,' and he made him ruler over all the land of Egypt" (Gn 41:41–43).

The psalmist said, "You made summer and winter and gave them to the earth" (Ps 74:17). The same God that made summer is the same God that made winter. The same God that blesses you in the summer can bless you in the winter season of your life. "To everything, there is a season, and a time to every purpose under the heaven" (Eccl 3:1). God wants us to bear fruit. God told Noah, "Be fruitful and multiply, and replenish the earth" (Gn 8:22). The word "fruitful" means "to grow or increase" (see Strong's #H6509).

God desires that we bear fruit. The Word of God says: "Blessed is the man that walketh not in the counsel of the ungodly, nor standeth in the way of sinners, nor sitteth in the seat of the scornful. But his delight is in the law of the Lord, and in his law doth he meditate day and night. And he shall be like a tree planted by the rivers of water, that bringeth forth his fruit in his season. His leaf also shall not wither, and whatsoever he doeth shall prosper" (Ps 1:1–3).

The life of Joseph illustrates a perfect storm. He was in the storm, and God caused him to prosper in the midst of it. The storm equipped Joseph to help his family and others. "Now no chastening for the present seemeth to be joyous, but grievous. Nevertheless afterward it yieldeth the peaceable fruit of righteousness unto them, which are exercised thereby" (Heb 12:11). When the winter was over, Solomon resorted to singing. Solomon said, "Winter is past, the rain has stopped. Flowers cover the earth, it is time to sing" (Song of Sg 2:11–12 CEV).

"Then shall we know, if we follow on to the *Lord,* his going forth is prepared as the morning; and he shall come unto us as the rain, as the latter and former rain unto the earth" (Hos 6:3).

This Is Only a Test

I can remember watching television, and my programming being interrupted. There would be a long beep, followed by the saying, "This is a test of the Emergency Broadcast System." The Emergency Broadcast System provides the public with a warning if there is a threat of war, severe weather, or storms.

Similarly, our own lives are sometimes momentarily interrupted. The tests of life have a way of clouding our vision. This is only temporary; seasons must change. It may seem as though you are in the storm and can't see your way out, but seasons must change. "For our light affliction, which is but for a moment, worketh for us a far more exceeding and eternal weight of glory. While we look not at the things which are not seen, for the things which are seen are temporal, but the things which are not seen are eternal (2 Cor 4:17–18).

Tom Bodett said, "The difference between school and life? In school, you're taught a lesson and then given a test. In life, you're given a test that teaches you a lesson."

Galatians 6:9 says, "And let us not be weary in well-doing, for in due season we shall reap, if we faint not." "To everything there is a season, and a time to every purpose under the heaven" (Eccl 3:1).

If God has given you a promise or a prophecy, you may have to wage war. First Timothy 1:18 says, "This charge I commit unto thee, son Timothy, according to the prophecies which went before on thee, that thou by them mightiest war a good warfare."

It is your responsibility to believe (take as being true or real) in the prophetic word spoken over your life. "Believe in the Lord your God, so shall ye be established; believe in his prophets, so shall you prosper" (2 Chr 20:20).

Some trials come to increase our faith. We won't know how much faith we have until we are tested. Job said, "But he knows what I am doing, and when he tests me, I will be pure as gold" (Jb 23:10 CEV).

For thousands of years, gold refiners have used the same process.

Chapter 13

GOD SPEAKS IN THE MIDST OF THE STORM

The storms of life can clearly be depicted in the prologue of the Book of Job. We read, "Behold, there came a great wind from the wilderness, and smote the four corners of the house" (Job 1:19). Job lost his health and wealth in one single day. In essence, he plummeted from the pinnacle of prosperity to the pit of despair. Job ultimately became the poster boy for the age-old mystery, "Why do bad things happen to good people?"

In the midst of Job's trials, "the Lord spoke to Job out of the storm" (Jb 38:1 NIV). God still speaks today in the midst of the storm. "Surely the Sovereign Lord does nothing without revealing his plan to his servants the prophets" (Am 3:7). He says, "For I know the plans I have for you . . . plans to prosper you and not to harm you, plans to give you peace and a future" (Jer 29:11).

Moreover, there were chapters in the Book of Job that I am sure Job wishes were not written. Similarly, there are chapters in our lives that we wish we could have skipped over. If we go to the last chapter of Job, we learn that "the Lord restored Job's losses . . . Indeed the Lord gave to Job twice as much as he had before . . . Now the Lord blessed the latter days of Job more than his beginning" (Jb 42:10, 12). We also have been through the storm and rain, but God declares, "For your shame ye shall receive double" (Is 61:7).

In the midst of Elijah's storm, there was a warrant out for him. "Elijah was afraid and ran for his life" (1 Kgs 19:3 NIV). Elijah suffered a brief bout of depression and thought he was all alone. Elijah, like so many of us, experienced great victories and many accomplishments. Prior to him being on the run, he had just had a mountaintop experience. Some of my deepest valleys were after my mountaintop experiences. I know what it is to be on the run and have to constantly look over your shoulder. I know what it feels like to stare at your home video camera monitors day and night. Elijah, like so many of us, cried out, "I have had enough, Lord" (1 Kgs 19:4).

God spoke to Elijah out of the storm. "The Lord said, 'Go out and stand on the mountain in the presence of the Lord, for the Lord is about to pass by.' Then a great and powerful wind tore the mountains apart and shattered the rocks before the Lord, but the Lord was not in the wind. After the wind there was an earthquake. After the earthquake came fire, but the Lord was not in the fire. After the fire came a gentle whisper" (1 Kgs 19:11–12).

As a result, when God speaks in the midst of your circumstances, He lets you know that you are not in this by yourself. He told Elijah there were, "seven thousand in Israel, all the knees which have not bowed to Baal." When God speaks, He gives you direction. God instructed Elijah to anoint his designated successor, and to anoint Jehu and Hazael as kings (see 1 Kgs 19).

God spoke in definite times, in definite ways. He spoke to Moses in the backside of the desert in a burning bush (Ex 3). He even opened the mouth of a donkey to speak and warn a prophet (Nm 22:29). God speaks in the midst of the storm and brings order out of darkness and chaos. In fact, the earth was formless and void, and God spoke the worlds into existence, and saw that it was good (Gn 1).

To demonstrate: "There arose a great storm of wind," and God spoke "and rebuked the wind, and said unto the sea, 'Peace, be still.' And there was a great calm." There was an old saying, "When E. F. Hutton talks, people listen," whereas when God speaks, He transforms your life and calms the storm.

In the midst of the storm, I was ordered by gunpoint into an abandoned garage. The gunman was only a few feet away from me when he pointed the gun at me and pulled the trigger. I thought it was over and could not believe it when I realized I was still standing and was not shot. Looking down the barrel of a gun, I began to plead for my life before he could pull the trigger again.

I left the garage and began to walk down a long alley. As I neared the end of the alley, the first thing my mind actually processed was a sticker on a parked car window that said "John 3:16." I began to think about that verse: "For God so loved the world that He sent His only begotten son that whosoever believeth in Him should not perish, but have everlasting life." By all rights, when that shot was fired at me, I should have perished, but I didn't.

I proceeded to walk a few more blocks to the house of someone I knew. They opened the door for me, and before I could even sit down, a little girl stared at me and began to yell at me. She said, "Charles, God is mad at you." I was still in a state of shock, and she continued to admonish me by the authority of God. She began to prophesy to me, saying, "You were supposed to go to the program." As she was yelling at me, I could still smell the gunpowder from the gunshot on my clothes. God was speaking to me in the midst of the storm.

In fact, I knew it was God because this little girl (Kayla) who was only about five or six years old had no way of knowing that I had been planning to go to Teen Challenge, a Christian-based treatment center. Furthermore, I never shared the experience of what happened in the garage with anyone at that time. It is written, "With praises from children and from tiny infants, you have built a fortress. It makes your enemies silent, and all who turn against you are left speechless" (Ps 8:2 CEV). When God speaks to you in the midst of the storm, it will leave you speechless.

Chapter 14

THE LONGEST WINTER

December 16, 1944 set the stage for what would become the narrative for Alex Kershaw's book, *The Longest Winter*. The book is about the Battle of the Bulge and the heroic real-life story of World War II's most declared platoon.

These men endured unfathomable, freezing temperatures, arctic blasts, frostbite, and firefights, all while getting hit with grenade shrapnel and machine gun fire. This was only the start of what would become their longest winter

They eventually ran out of ammunition, surrendering and ultimately becoming prisoners of war. Imprisoned, they endured brutal treatment, surgeries without anesthetic, and starvation. The POWs defined the phrase "hungry as a hostage" as they scribbled fantasy recipes on scratch paper. They were eventually rescued by General George Patton.

December 25, 2007, marked a bitter, cold day in history that I will never forget. I was marched through a snowy alleyway by my captor. Meteorologists recorded wind gusts of 22 miles per hour and my visibility was near zero. By all accounts, I was in the midst of the storm. Immediately I was ordered into a dark garage, and the enemy came in. Isaiah 59:19 says, "When the enemy shall come in like a flood, the spirit of the Lord shall lift up a standard against him."

All of a sudden, I saw a flash of lightning and heard a thunderous roar as my life flashed before my eyes. Miraculously, despite the gunmen's close range, I was not riddled with bullets. God says, "Behold, I myself have created the smith [Smith & Wesson] who blows the fire of coals and brings out a weapon . . . No weapon that is formed against you shall prosper" (Is 54:16–17 NASB, emphasis mine).

Notwithstanding, the enemy didn't know I had some comrades on the frontline. I had a praying grandmother who was a prayer warrior, and a soldier in the army of the Lord. By grace I was saved through faith, and not of myself. It was a gift of God (see Eph 2:8–9). I walked out of the abandoned garage (tomb) down that long alley with one set of footprints in the snow, knowing God had carried me through the longest winter.

December 2016, Winter Storms Aaron and Bailey brought about insane windchill factors, freezing rains, black ice, and subzero temperatures. Thirty-three states were under severe weather alerts, thousands of flights were canceled, and tens of millions were slammed hard by heavy snow.

Let's check the weather in your neck of the woods. While meteorologists and climatologists say that winter begins on December 21 and ends on March 20, someone reading this will say, "I feel like I'm experiencing the longest winter." I have an avalanche of bills, and I'm getting the cold shoulder in my relationship. Someone else's winter may be putting Peruvian flakes up their nose while someone else's medical forecast may be cloudy. In all the research I gathered about weather in writing this book, I learned that seasons must change. "To everything there is a season, and a time to every purpose under heaven" (Eccl 3:1).

Peradventure, like the Battle of the Bulge, there is a war going on. "For the weapons of our warfare are not carnal but mighty through God, to the pulling down of strongholds. Casting down imaginations and every high thing that exalts itself against the knowledge of God, and bringing into captivity every thought to obedience of Christ" (2 Cor 10:45).

A point often overlooked is that when God has given you a promise or prophecy for your life, the enemy comes in and tries to halt or steal the plan. "The thief cometh not, but for to kill, steal, and destroy" (Jn 10:10). For this reason, Paul admonishes Timothy, "This change I commit to you, son Timothy, according to the prophecies previously made concerning you, that by them you may wage a good warfare" (1 Tm 1:18 NKJV)

Finally, my brethren, be strong in the Lord, and in the power of His might. Put on the whole armor of God that ye may be able to stand against the wiles of the devil.

"For we wrestle not against flesh and blood but against principalities, against powers, against the rulers of darkness of this world, and against spiritual wickedness in high places. Wherefore take unto you the whole armor of God, that ye may be able to stand in the evil day, and having done all to stand, to stand" (Eph 6:10–14).

Angels in the Snow

The first snow angel was invented by Anna Thomas in 1904. She had fallen, and when she got up, she saw that she had made an angel figure. Making snow angels has commonly become a childhood game. In fact, Green Bay Packers player Randall Cobb scored a touchdown and celebrated by lying down and making a snow angel.

Notably, I can hear my mother saying, "God has got these angels." The psalmist says, "For He shall give His angels charge over thee, to keep thee in all thy ways" (Ps 91:11).

As an illustration, Elisha was surrounded by the Syrian army. There were "horses and chariots and a strong force." Elisha reassured his servant not to worry, for "those are with us and more who are with them" (2 Kgs 6:16 NIV). Then Elisha prayed, "Lord, open his eyes so that he may see" (2 Kgs 6:20 NIV). When the Lord opened his eyes, "he looked and saw horses and chariots of fire all around Elisha" (2 Kgs 6:20).

They saw legions of heaven at Elisha's disposal. The enemy was powerless. Psalms 68:17 confirms "chariots of God are tens of thousands and thousands upon thousands." God "maketh his angels spirits; his ministers a flaming fire" (Ps 104:4).

In other words, we may feel small or outnumbered in the face of our enemies, but "if God be for us, then who can be against us?" (Rom 8:31). There are more of us than there are of them. God has got these angels. When you fall in the snow, snow storms of life, pray that God opens your eyes to see the angels in the snow.

Daniel was praying and fasting and confessing that Babylon had fallen into sin. The angel came to Daniel, saying, "Do not fear, Daniel. From the first day you set your heart to understand, and to humble yourself before God, your words were heard. I have come because of your words" (Dn 10:12). He went on to notify Daniel that the enemy had been interfering, but Michael the chief angel came to help.

In these given points throughout history, we note that men, women, and children alike have fallen, both great and small. Dating back from 539 BC, when Babylon fell into Babylonian captivity, to that little girl that made the first snow angel in 1904, and to date. "For all have sinned and fallen short of the glory of God" (Rom 3:23). "If we confess our sins, He is faithful and will cleanse us from all unrighteousness" (1 Jn 1:9). When David committed adultery, he said, "Wash me, and I shall be whiter than snow" (Ps 51).

In short, seasons are an inevitable part of life. Remember that if you ever experience what seems to be the longest winter.

One writer notes, in every season, of course, storms may appear. You may be dancing on a sunbeam when the ring of the telephone comes like a clap of thunder, bearing unexpected news of calamity—or loss, period. Even the best seasons of life can be clouded by a storm.

At such times, thank God for the promise in His word, that wonderful phrase of Scripture found 120 times in 120 verses, or ten times for each month: "It shall come to pass." Storms come, and storms pass. They don't last forever. The sun will shine again!

The passing years and seasons, I've found, have galvanized my emotions. I know now that not every storm will sink my ship. (Hopefully none of them will!) I also know that when the storm is raging, my feelings are not sure ground.

I take heart in God's commandments to Job, the man of many seasons, that serial storms have boundless lessons. There are treasures in the snow, God told Job, and hail is reserved for the days of trouble, wars, and battle. I have learned that today's tempest often will hold the sustenance and strength for the future. Storms can make channels for the rain, and tender new growth comes as a result of the storm (see Jb 38:22–23, 25–27).

Paul said we comfort others "with the comfort which we ourselves are comforted by God" (2 Cor 1:4). The increasing fruitfulness of subsequent seasons, from which we nurture others, may often be augmented by the experience of a storm.

So whatever season of life you are in, make full use of it! Even a dormant season can become a special time for needed rest, quiet listening to God, and fresh study. Don't waste time wishing you were someone else, somewhere else, doing something else. This is a futile exercise. God made you as you are to use you as He planned. Living fully in your present is the best insurance for your future.

Understanding the law of seasons can relieve whatever pressure you feel about your current circumstances and increase your faith for the future. While we anticipate the fruit, we must understand the process. You will bring forth fruit in due season (see Ps 1:13). Don't despair; the day of reaping will come!

Chapter 15

YOUR BEST IS YET TO COME

You haven't seen anything yet! Your best is yet to come! In 1 Corinthians 2:9, the apostle Paul says, "But as it is written, eye hath not seen, nor ear heard, neither have entered into the heart of man, the things which God hath prepared for them that love Him." You haven't seen anything yet; your best days are yet ahead. It doesn't matter how old you are, don't worry about your biological clock. The Word of God says, "And I will restore all the years" (Jl 2:25). It doesn't matter what it looks like, your best is yet to come.

The Gospel narrative according to John contains a series of miracles. The first is the transformation of water to wine in Cana. John 2 tells the story of the wedding at Cana. In John 2:1–11, we learn of Jesus's first miracle:

"Three days later, Mary, the mother of Jesus, was at a wedding feast in the village of Cana in Galilee. Jesus and His disciples had also been invited and were there.

"When the wine was all gone, Mary said to Jesus, 'They don't have any more wine.' Jesus replied, 'Mother, my time hasn't yet come! You must not tell me what to do.'

"Mary then said to the servants, 'Do whatever Jesus tells you to do.'

Those who threw the feast were prepared and had calculated how much they would need to satisfy the guests, but they were in it longer than they expected. Sometimes you can be in a storm longer than you expected. You also can be prepared, and things can still run out. Prominent financial advisors teach us that our savings should be equal to our total expenses for at least several months, just in case an unexpected misfortune happens like losing your job, becoming injured in a car accident, and so on.

Those that were in charge of the feast ran out, even though they thought they were prepared. Even though Jesus was on the scene, they still ran out. I am here to tell you that you can run out of some things even with Jesus there. Just because I am going through things, just because I'm in the midst of the storm, doesn't mean that I don't have Jesus. The gifts and callings of God are without repentance. Some people believe that if you are going through things, "it's because of your sin." Contrary to popular belief, the Bible says:

"There was a man who lived in the land of Uz. His name was Job. He was honest. He did what was right. He had respect for God and avoided evil. Yet one day a messenger came to him, told him lightning fell from the sky and destroyed his possessions, and that a strong wind blew from the desert and shattered his family" (Jb 1:1).

In spite of everything, Job did not sin. Just because you are going through the storm does not mean that Jesus is not with you; He is in the boat with you. The disciples were in the midst of the storm, and Jesus was yet present. We know that in all things, God works for the good of those who love Him.

He will do it sooner than you expect; those at the party did not know he was capable of performing miracles. He had not performed any miracles before this. John 2:11 says, "This beginning of signs Jesus did in Cana of Galilee, and manifested himself and His glory; and His disciples believed in Him." However, his mother knew she was a virgin when she gave birth to Him, which was a miracle by itself. The mother of Jesus goes on to say to Him, "They have no wine." Nevertheless, according to the Messianic timetable, Jesus was on a schedule. Jesus said unto her, "Woman, does your concern have to do with me? My hour has not yet come." Jesus was not yet ready to reveal himself, but because of faith, he revealed himself. If you put your faith in Jesus, He will do it sooner than expected. Your faith will cause Jesus to do it sooner The eyes of the Lord are looking to and fro for someone to show Himself strong on their behalf.The very fact that they ran out meant that they had to rely solely on Jesus. I am sure that when they tasted the wine, they thought to themselves, "I'm glad I ran out, taste and see that the Lord is good." "You have kept the best until last." Sometimes you can't see God until you run out yourself. There used to be a saying that said we do more by 6:00 a.m. than we do all day. I'm here to tell you, that which would have sometimes taken years in my own strength to accomplish, God has done for me instantly. I'm sure someone is glad they ran out of money to pay the rent, because had they not run out of rent money, they would not be living in the beautiful home they are living in now. If that boss hadn't run out of patience with me, I would not be the boss now, or I wouldn't have been promoted elsewhere. If that car had not run out, I would not be driving this one.

First Kings 17 tells the story of Elijah who had just received word that there would be no rain for the next few years. God commanded him to go to Kerith Valley, east of the Jordan River, where God commanded the ravens to bring him bread and meat to eat.

He also drank water from the brook. Sometime later, the brook ran out because "it hadn't rained in the land for quite a while." I'm sure you know from experience, you never miss your water until your well runs out.

Conversely, when God gets ready to bless you, He begins to move things out of your way to make room for the new blessing. The Bible tells the story of the widow at Zarephath who was about to run out of food. She was down to her last meal and told the prophet Elijah, "All I have is a small amount of flour in a jar and a little olive oil in a jug. I'll make one last meal myself and my son. We'll eat it, and after that, we'll die."[9] Nonetheless, she was obedient to the man of God, and shared her last meal. Even so, when she ran out, God continued to miraculously provide for her.

When Elijah ran out of food, God did the miraculous and commanded the ravens to feed him. Considering that God does the miraculous when you run out, aren't you glad that you have run out of some things? God saves the best for last.

At the feast there were six stone water jars that were used by the people for washing themselves in the way that their religion said they must. Each jar held about twenty or thirty gallons. Jesus told the servants to fill them to the top with water. Then after the jars had been filled, He said, "Now take some water and give it to the man in charge of the feast."

The servants did as Jesus told them, and the man in charge drank some of the water that had now turned into wine. He did not know where the wine had come from, but the servants did. He called the bridegroom over and said, "The best wine is always served first." Then, after guests have had plenty, the other wine was served. "*But you have kept the best until last!*" (Jn 2:1–10).

This was Jesus's first miracle, and He did it in the village of Cana in Galilee. There Jesus showed His glory, and His disciples put their faith in Him (Jn 2:11).

The person in charge said, "The best wine is always served first. Then after guests have had plenty, the other wine is served." Interestingly, this is how nightclubs make their money. They start out serving strong drinks, and then when people have become drunk, they begin to water down the drinks. The devil also operates by giving us the best first, and then that which is worse.

The world system teaches us that to be successful, we have to own a house with a white picket fence, have a personal income of $42,693 per year, send our children to private schools, and own 2.28 vehicles per household. The Greek word "world" is Strong's #3625 *kosmos,* which means "orderly arrangement." We can see the same word explained in Ephesians: "Wherein in time past ye walked according to the course of this world, according to the prince of the power of the air [the devil], the spirit that now worketh in the children of disobedience" (Eph 3:3, emphasis mine). We have to understand that there is the world's system and God's system.

The person in charge of the feast goes on to say, "But you have kept the best until last" (Jn 2:10). We can learn from Jesus's first miracle that He saves the best for last. In biblical interpretation, there is a Bible study method called the law of first mention. What this law basically says is that anytime we see something mentioned for the first time in the Bible, we should pay very close attention to it because it sets the stage for following Scriptures.

I believe that He wanted us to know that His ways are not our ways, that He doesn't follow the world's system, and that He saves the best for last. It doesn't matter what it looks like, promotion comes from God. The Word of God says, "Remember ye not the former things, neither consider the things of old. Behold, I will do a new thing; now it shall spring forth. Shall ye not know it? I will even make a way in the wilderness, and rivers in the desert" (Is 43:18–19).

The Bible tells the story of the prodigal son:

"Jesus continued, 'There was a man who had two sons. The younger son spoke to his father. He said, 'Father, give me my share of the family property.' So the father divided his property between his two sons.

"Not long after that, the younger son packed up all he had. Then he left for a country far away. There he wasted his money on wild living. He spent everything he had.

"Then the whole country ran low on food, so the son didn't have what he needed. He went to work for someone who lived in that country, who sent him to the fields to feed the pigs. The son wanted to fill his stomach with the food the pigs were eating, but no one gave him anything.

"Then he began to think clearly again. He said, 'How many of my father's hired workers have more than enough food! But here I am dying from hunger! I will get up and go back to my father. I will say to him, 'Father, I have sinned against heaven. And I have sinned against you. I am no longer fit to be called your son. Make me like one of your hired workers.'

"While the son was still a long way off, his father saw him. He was filled with tender love for his son. He ran to him. He threw his arms around him and kissed him.

"The son said to him, 'Father, I have sinned against heaven and against you. I am no longer fit to be called your son.'

"But the father said to his servants, 'Quick! Bring the best robe and put it on him. Put a ring on his finger and sandals on his feet. Bring the fattest calf and kill it. Let's have a big dinner and celebrate'" (Lk 15:11–23 NIV).

We can learn from the prodigal son that it doesn't matter what you have been through, we have a father that is waiting to give us His best! The prodigal son came to his senses, *"While the son was still a long way off, his father saw him. He was filled with tender love for his son. He ran to him. He threw his arms around him and kissed him.* The father said, 'Quick! Bring the *best* robe and put it on him. Put a ring on his finger and sandals on his feet. Bring the fattest calf and kill it. Let's have a big dinner and celebrate'" (Lk 15:11–23 NIV).

The prodigal son started out saying, *"Father, give me"* (Lk 15:12), and later said, *"Make me like one of your hired workers"* (Lk 15:19 NIV). We have to come to the place where we begin to say, "Lord, make me over. You're the potter and I'm the clay. I want your best for my life."

"Now unto him that is able to do exceeding abundantly above all that we ask or think, according to the power that worketh in us" (Eph 3:20).

Final Word

THE STORM IS OVER NOW

Picking up the Pieces

After a storm, tens of thousands are ultimately left with the painstaking task of picking up the pieces. Hurricane Matthew brought enormous amounts of rain and floodwaters. Water rescue crews used helicopters and boats to rescue residents. President Obama signed a disaster declaration.

Nichols is a Mayberry-like town in South Carolina. Nichols is positioned between two convening rivers, which caused it to fill up like a giant bathtub. Water, fuel, and sewage swept through all the nearby homes and towns, leaving them inhabitable. The majority of residents didn't even have flood insurance. A lifetime's worth of furniture and belongings were piled along the streets. One resident became emotional as he mentioned the family photos. He stated, "I'm fine except when I talk about the family photos." When the floodwaters finally receded, homes were covered in toxic black mold and sewage. The town's churches and businesses were also flooded. Many of the residents and parishioners began the arduous task of picking up the pieces.

In comparison, many of us have endured the storms of life, but we've got to get back up! There is a Japanese proverb that says, "Fall seven times, stand up eight." We can't continue to sit and watch life pass us by. Some reports have estimated that the life expectancy of a woman is seventy-eight years, and even lower for men. That's only about 941 months.

A famine besieged Samaria, and there were four leprous men sitting, "and they said one to another, 'Why sit here until we die? If we say we will enter the city, then the famine [storm] is in the city, and we shall die there. And if we sit still here, we die also.' And they rose up in the twilight" (2 Kgs 7:3–5, emphasis mine). Twilight is the darkest hour. You've got to rise up; I don't care how dark your situation may be. Those lepers made up their mind that they were going to pick up the pieces, despite sickness, poverty, an avalanche of criticism, and being labeled as outcasts.

In the midst of the storm, those lepers got up and "came to the uttermost part of the camp. They went into one tent, and did eat and drink, and carried thence silver and gold and raiment" (2 Kgs 7:8). Micah 7:8 says, "Rejoice not against me, O mine enemy: when I fall, I shall arise, and when I sit in darkness, the Lord shall be a light unto me." An American proverb says, "Our greatest glory consists not in never falling, but in rising every time we fall."

Interestingly, the English word for crisis means "time of difficulty and of anxious waiting." However, the Chinese word for crisis means both danger and opportunity. In essence, it means that we can go through the storms (crises) of life and turn them into opportunities. Albert Einstein said, "In the middle of difficulty lies opportunity."

The Russian River flooded about 650 homes in Guerneville, California. There was a woman named Loris Doelman, who saw this storm or flood as an opportunity to go kayaking in her home. She was featured on *World News* holding paddles and rowing smoothly on a kayak through her living room which was filled with water. Pictures could be seen on the walls high above the water. Walls turned sideways are bridges. She was putting into action a quote by Louisa May Alcott, which stated, "I am not afraid of storms, for I am learning to sail my ship."

We have got to pick up the pieces through the storm and rain. It doesn't matter if you are literally underground in the Oklahoma State Penitentiary, locked up on Rikers Island in New York, in the crack house or the White House, rich or poor, young or old. In the words of George Eliot, "It's never too late to be what you might have been."

Perfect example: ninety-nine-year-old Doreetha Daniels graduated from college with a degree in science. She endured the unfathomable watershed moments in history including the Great Depression, World War II, and the civil rights movement. *USA Today* stated, "Doreetha is a living testament to the saying, 'If there is a will, there is a way.'" In a statement to KTLA 5, Doreetha

Daniels advised others, "Don't give up. Don't let anybody discourage you. Say that 'I'm going to do it,' and do it for yourself."

Peradventure, there comes a time in the life of every reader of this book that you will be required to pick up the pieces of your life. In the midst of the storm, David returned home and found that it was burned down to the ground. His wives and children were carried away captive, and those with him spoke of stoning him. However, "David encouraged himself in the Lord his God." David picked up the pieces, got up, and went to the enemy's camp, "and David recovered all" (see Sm 30). We have to begin to change our perception of the storm. For example, if you look through a telescope, things seem larger than life. However, if you turn a telescope around and look through the other end, the atmosphere and storms seems smaller. To an ant, a few drops of rain is a flood. ABC News reported "storms producing heavy downpours could increase 400 percent by 2100." "When the enemy shall come in like a flood, the Spirit of the Lord shall lift up a standard "(Is 59:19).

The Cross

In the heart of the Bible belt, in Moore, Oklahoma, drywall, boards, glass, nails, shingles, tattered wood, furnishings, rubble, and debris were piled far above the ground against the Moore First Baptist Church. A fierce tornado demolished a nearby subdivision, but caused slight damage to the house of worship. Unexpectedly, a generator motor revved up, and all of a sudden, the rescue lights flashed on and brightly illuminated the church's 50-foot cross which was located on top of a dark hill.

The fire chief set up an emergency command center outside the church, and people were attending to the wounded in the dark. In the interim, the soaring cross continued shining brilliantly through the black storm clouds. In the midst of the storm, over one hundred thousand people were without electricity, and natural gas lines leaked all over the city. Hundreds of people were coming across the road and were pointing to the place of worship as an assistant pastor was saying, "Go to the cross, go to the cross." The injured and misplaced screamed, cried, and hobbled to the cross, in the same way a large crowd that followed Jesus thousands of years ago mourned and lamented as they followed Him to Calvary. The cross is a safe haven, and has been a refuge for people throughout history. "The message of the cross seems foolish to those who are lost and dying. But it is God's power to us who are being saved."

Jonah was in a storm, "and such a bad storm came up that the ship was about to broken in to pieces" (Jon 1:4 CEV). The Bible says, "Then Jonah prayed . . . And said, 'I cried by reason of mine affliction unto the Lord, and He heard me. Out of the belly of hell cried I, and Thou heardest my voice.' And the Lord spake unto the fish, and it vomited out Jonah upon the dry land" (Jon 2:1–2, 7).

Many people have compared prison to being in the belly of the whale. Jonah made a vow while he was in the fish. Likewise, we make vows while we are going through the storms of life. We may have said, "Lord, if you bring me out of this, l will serve you."

The Word of the Lord came to Jonah the second time and told him to go preach unto Nineveh. "So Jonah arose, and went unto Nineveh, according to the Word of the Lord. Now Nineveh was an exceeding great city of three days' journey. And Jonah began to enter the city a days' journey" (Jon 3:3). When Jonah was delivered from the storm, he didn't waste any time getting to business. It was three days' journey, but Jonah made it in one. Tell yourself, "I'm corning out with my hands up. I thank God for bringing me out, I will keep my vow."

A Missouri man was wrongfully convicted of a crime and spent a decade of his life in prison. The Supreme Court totally exonerated him and said that he was innocent. His attorney boldly wrote the words "It is over" on the back of a book and surprised him by placing the back of the book on the window of the prison room the man was in so that he could read it. He was in a storm, yet when he saw those words, he said he knew it was over. Note that in the Bible, being released from prison provides a picture of restoration.

As I was writing this final thought, the news media outlets aired his press conference and interviews. As I watched the interview, he had the book with him that his attorney had written the words on. He held the book up, and I could see the words "It is over" written on the back. As I write the last thought on the back of this book, I want you to know, It is over. Hold this book up like the man that spent a decade in prison, and say, "It is over." That storm that you have been going through, "It is over!" As I explained earlier in this book, some storms are simply man-made storms, and the power of life and death are in the power of the tongue. Begin to call the things that are not, as though they are. Open your mouth and begin to speak the words, "It is over."

I thank God for changing my prison garments and causing me to be fruitful in my land of affliction (in the midst of the storm). I learned that God will give you peace in the midst of the storm—not in its absence, but in spite of it. In closing, I would like to echo the words of Gospel singer and songwriter Kurt Franklin: "I feel that I can make it, the storm is over now."

To contact the author for bookings: Inthemidstofthestorm@aol.com

ABOUT THE AUTHOR

Charles Dickens received his honorary degree from the school of hard knocks. Through his life experiences, firsthand knowledge, inspirational messages, and books, he is able to deliver a commencement speech to encourage others.

In addition, he is a college graduate, a certified credit counselor, a certified trainer of Evangelism Explosion, and a degree holder from Anchor Theological Seminary and Bible Institute.

Charles Dickens has been presented with numerous certifications and awards in various fields of study.

He has also volunteered on panels to help at-risk youth and to help prisoners gain employability skills. He enjoys encouraging others and teaching financial literacy.

Charles Dickens currently resides in Wisconsin.

STUDY GUIDE

"Study *and* do your best to present yourself to God, approved a workman [tested by trial] who has no reason to be ashamed, accurately handling *and* skillfully teaching the word of truth." (2 Tim 2:15 AMP)

The purpose of this study guide is to assist the reader in applying biblical principles to their life while pushing them to greater heights. This section contains a variety of questions about the book and the Scriptures that cause the reader to dig deeper while applying biblical truths and principles to their lives.

This reader's guide may be used for personal or group study.

OUTLINE

1. In the introduction, the author alludes to Habakkuk 2:3, where God told Habakkuk to "write the vision." The author also noted the importance of writing things down, as experts suggest you are 70 percent more likely to remember it. Write down one thing that God has promised you or you want to accomplish in your life.

2. Storms arise in our personal lives, not with the purpose of defeating us or forcing us to take shelter (isolation), but as a catalyst to push us to a new level. What storms of life have you experienced in the past? How have those storms benefited you positively?

3. In the introduction, the author notes that many of us can be faced with what seems to be insurmountable circumstances, just like in the life of David. In the midst of the storm, David said, "Oh that I had wings like a dove, for then I would fly away and be at rest . . . from the windy storm and the tempest." Have the storms of life ever had you wishing you were someone else, somewhere else, doing something else? If so, what Scriptures can you meditate on to remove those negative thoughts?

4. In chapter one, "Praise God in the Midst of the Storm," the author notes: V. Raymond Edman said, "Never doubt in the darkness what God has told you in the light." What dreams or visions has God shown or told you for your life? Have you given up hope because they have not come to fruition?

5. In chapter two, "That's Crazy," we learned how God "has chosen the foolish things of the world to confound the wise." What totally amazing thing has God done in your life where you would have to ultimately say, "That's crazy"?

6. In chapter six, "Highs and Lows," the author notes that First Lady Michelle Obama talked about lessons that she and the president try to teach their daughters. "How we explain when someone is cruel or acts like a bully, you don't stoop to their level. No, our motto is: 'When they go low, we go high.'" What lessons can we learn from her powerful speech?

7. In chapter eight, "Pray in the Midst of the Storm," the author talks about the prayer of agreement. Matthew 18:19 says, "Again I say unto you, that if two of you shall agree on earth as touching anything they shall ask, it shall be one for them of my father in heaven." Do you have a prayer partner you can touch and agree with? What answers to prayer have you experienced as a result of the prayer of agreement?

8. In chapter ten, "Standing on the Word in the Midst of the Storm," the author notes that that there are 783,000 words in the Bible and 3,573 promises. Which one Scripture will you commit to personalize, visualize, and ultimately memorize? For example, Romans 8:31: "If God be for us, who can be against us?"

    Personalize: If God be for me, who can be against me?
    Visualize: Visualize God fighting your battles, making good on His promises, and so on.
    Memorize: Commit the selected Scripture to memory.

9. What is the one fascinating fact, biblical principle, or thing that you have learned from this book, which you can apply to your personal life?

10. Read 2 Chronicles 20:1–25.

    A. What victories did Jehosophat gain by being obedient and praising God?
    B. What was the promise made to Jehosophat? (Verse 17)
    C. What victories can you obtain by being obedient and praising God in the midst of the storm?

11. In chapter nine, "Sow in the Midst of the Storm," we learned from Isaac's example how to trust God in the area of our finances, even in a famine or storm.
    We read: "And there was a famine [storm] in the land besides the first famine that was in the days of Abraham . . . Then Isaac sowed in that land [storm] and received in the same year a hundredfold. And the Lord blessed him" (Gn 26:1, 12, emphasis mine). Also, the Amplified Bible Book of Ecclesiastes 11:4 says, "He who observes the wind [and waits for all conditions to be favorable] will not sow, and he who regards the clouds will not reap."

    A. How can you sow your finances in the midst of the storm?
    B. How can you sow your time, talents, and abilities to help others, even in the midst of your own personal storms?

12. Describe how the phrase, quote, and Scripture listed below has impacted or can be implemented in your life.

    • The Chinese word for crisis means both danger and opportunity

- "In the middle of difficulty lies opportunity." – Albert Einstein
- "And we know all things work together for good to them that love God, to them who are called according to his purpose" (Rom 8:28).

13. After the storm, tens of thousands are left with the painstaking task of picking up the pieces. During this process, sometimes individuals have to tear down and rebuild their lives.

   A. What negative or self-defeating thoughts do you have to tear down in your life?
   B. What positive thoughts can you use to replace the old negative ones? (See 2 Corinthians 10:3–5).

END NOTES

1. www.chacha.com/question/who invented snow angel

2. Thetus Tenney. *Seeking the Savior* (Family Christian Stores, 2003), pp. 90–91.

Personal Journal

"Write down for the coming generations what the Lord has done, so that people not yet born will praise Him." (Psalms 102:18 TEV)

WRITE DOWN YOUR PRAISE REPORTS

_____

_____

_____

_____

_____

_____

_____

_____

_____

_____

_____

_____

_____

"Oh that my words were now written! Oh that they were printed in a book!" (Job 19:23)

_____

_____

_____

_____

_____

_____

_____

_____

_____

_____

_____

_____

_____

_____

_____

"And this is the confidence [the assurance, the privilege of boldness] which we have in Him: [We are sure] that if we ask anything [make any requests] according to His will [an agreement with His own plan], He listens and hears us. And if we [positively] know that He listens to us in whatever we ask, we also know [with settled, absolute knowledge] that we have [granted us as our present possessions] the request made of Him." (1 Jn 5:14–15).

WRITE DOWN YOUR PRAYER REQUESTS

"I will answer their prayers before they finish praying." (Is 65:24 CEV)

WRITE DOWN YOUR ANSWERS TO PRAYER

_____

_____

_____

_____

_____

_____

_____

_____

_____

_____

_____

_____

_____

_____

_____

_____

"These things I plan won't happen right away. Slowly, steadily, surely the time approaches when the vision will be fulfilled. If it seems slow, do not despair, for these things will surely come to pass. Just be patient! They will not be overdue a single day!" (Hb 2:3 Living Bible).
"WRITE THE VISION [YOUR DREAMS AND VISIONS] AND MAKE IT PLAIN." (Habakkuk 2:2)

Other Resources

To receive an autographed copy of this five-star book with a 20 percent discount, visit us at www.
authorcharlesdickens.com.

The Bible mentions money and property more than 2,300 times. Moreover, the book of Hosea says, "My people are destroyed for lack of knowledge."

It is estimated that over eighty million Americans are living with poor credit, and recent studies have shown that up to 79 percent of all credit reports contain errors. Use this recession-proof guerilla repair guide to quickly and legally repair your credit and improve your scores. Don't pay credit repair companies thousands of dollars; do it yourself and be fast on your way to owning the car or house of your dreams.

Printed in the United States
By Bookmasters